Divorce Proofing Your Marriage

Divorce Proofing Your Marriage

Linda Mintle, Ph.D.

SILOAM PRESS

Living in Health—Body, Mind and Spirit

DIVORCE PROOFING YOUR MARRIAGE by Linda Mintle, Ph.D.
Published by Siloam Press
A part of Strang Communications Company
600 Rinehart Road
Lake Mary, Florida 32746
www.siloampress.com

Unless otherwise noted, all Scripture quotations are from the
New King James Version of the Bible. Copyright © 1979, 1980,
1982 by Thomas Nelson, Inc., publishers. Used by permission.

Scripture quotations marked TLB are from The Living Bible.
Copyright © 1971. Used by permission of Tyndale House
Publishers, Inc., Wheaton, IL 60189. All rights reserved.

Author's Note: All references to clients in this book come
from my clinical experience over the past twenty years of
conducting therapy in various states and settings around the
country. Names, places and other identifying details have been
changed and altered to protect the privacy and anonymity of the
individuals to whom they refer. Many case examples are
composites of a number of clients who share similar issues and
are equally protected with name and information changes to
remain confidential. Any similarity between the names and
stories of individuals described in this book and individuals
known to readers is coincidental and not intentional.

Interior design by Pat Theriault
Cover design by Rachel Campbell

Library of Congress Catalog Card Number: 2001087161
International Standard Book Number: 0-88419-732-8

01 02 03 04 05   8 7 6 5 4 3 2 1
Printed in the United States of America

Dedication

To Norm, my husband of twenty-six years: You have been the model of Christ in this relationship. Your unfailing love overwhelms me. Marrying you was the best decision I ever made. I love you.

To my parents, Bill and Esther Marquardt, who modeled an egalitarian relationship before it was culturally popular: You were the prototype for how a professional man and woman can live together and raise a family. Your fifty-six years of marriage is an accomplishment. Gary, Dennis and I were blessed to grow up in a family in which divorce was never an option or a thought. We've survived tribulations–cancer, comas, the untimely death of my brother and your son, infertility, failing health and more. I never doubted we would make it as a family.

To my aunts and uncles (six on Dad's side and seven on Mom's) who have also proven that marriage can last a lifetime with one partner: You have provided a legacy of marriage–not divorce.

To my in-laws, Harold and Bea Mintle: You have demonstrated God's power through your fifty-one years together. I have watched how God's grace and mercy have been sufficient and how a strong foundation built on God's Word eventually overcomes. Thanks for being loving and prayerful in-laws.

To all the couples who have honored their covenants and intimately allowed me a place in their lives: Thank you for teaching me and reminding me that marriage is a holy union held together by God.

Acknowledgments

Writing a book is an impossible task without people who love and support you. This has been an incredibly busy season in my life. It was only through the unwavering support of my husband that I even finished this project. Thank you, Norm, for running kids to ballet, soccer and church events in order to provide me time to write. Thanks for your excellent input in editing the manuscript. You are incredible.

Thanks, Matt and Katie, for understanding that Mom needed time to write. You guys were never an interruption—only a joy. The countdown is over! Now we go back to "regular Mom stuff."

Thanks to Rick Nash for help in developing this book. You are missed.

Thanks to the Siloam Press team, especially Dave Welday and Barbara Dycus, for all the work and effort put into this project.

Contents

Introduction
Divorce-Proofing Your Marriage—*xi*
10 Lies That Lead to Divorce–
10 Truths That Will Prevent It

1 **Lies, Lies and More Lies—1**
Seduced

2 **Three Key Preconditions to Divorce-Proofing—11**
Ready, Set, Go

3 **Escape and Avoidance—21**
Lie #1   Marriage is a contract.
Truth #1   Marriage is a covenant designed by God.

4 **Family Matters—41**
Lie #2   I married you, not your family!
Truth #2   You don't marry only your spouse–you get
              a package deal.

5 **Rescue Fantasies—63**
Lie #3   I can change my spouse.
Truth #3   You can change only your part in the
              dance.

6 **Dealing With Conflict—85**
Lie #4   We are too different.
Truth #4   Incompatibility or differences do not kill a
              relationship. How you work out those
              differences is what counts.

7 **Growing Apart—109**

Lie #5   I've lost that loving feeling, and it's gone, gone, gone!

Truth #5   That loving feeling can be restored.

8 **Gender Relations—135**

Lie #6   A more traditional marriage will save us.

Truth #6   God's intention is gender equality.

9 **Power Outage—155**

Lie #7   I can't change–this is who I am; take it or leave it.

Truth #7   I can change, but it requires desire, obedience and power.

10 **Infidelity—181**

Lie #8   There has been an affair. We need to divorce.

Truth #8   Affairs are serious and damaging, but not beyond repair and reconciliation.

11 **Cheap Grace—203**

Lie #9   It doesn't matter what I do; God will forgive me.

Truth #9   Receive God's grace with a repentant heart.

12 **Nothing Is Impossible—219**

Lie #10   It's too broken. Nothing can fix this relationship.

Truth #10   It's never too late because nothing is impossible with God.

Notes—239

Divorce-Proofing Your Marriage

10 Lies That Lead to Divorce— 10 Truths That Will Prevent It

Relationships are hard work. Conflict arises. Stress abounds. People problem-solve differently. Values vary. Expectations aren't always realistic. And let's face it, most of us are still trying to figure out who we are and what we need—much less how to deal with another person.

Even so, we move through life longing for that perfect mate. While intimacy with God is our ultimate aim, we also desire the human experience of intimacy. Once we find our lifelong partner, the task is to build and sustain a relationship over the years. For many couples, that is an uphill battle. Either true intimacy never develops, or it breaks down over time. This book is designed to prevent that breakdown.

Too many couples divorce over fixable problems. The

numbers alarm me. Fixable problems usually involve two people who stop liking each other and grow apart. Living in today's world, it is easy to become confused about who we are and how our relationships are supposed to work. Our spiritual foundations are shaky and full of cracks. When pressure comes, we crumble. We don't know what to believe or what to do.

People who divorce often say, "I never thought it would happen to me." No one wants divorce to happen. Few people marry believing it will. But it does, and the fallout is painful.

This is a book about preventing divorce. It is not meant to condemn those who are already divorced. When people decide they no longer want to be married, something has motivated them to make that decision. The reasons they want out vary, but all have one common thread—lies and deception have infiltrated their thinking. These lies involve the self, the other and God. Once a lie takes hold, destruction ultimately follows.

This book is not a marriage manual or a neatly packaged program to teach you new techniques. This is an all-out frontal attack on the very thing that often leads to divorce—lies: Lies that are birthed in our culture and absorbed into our thinking; lies that go against the truth of God; lies that grip our minds and play out in relationships, so much so that over time, we don't even recognize that we have been deceived.

I am writing to you from two perspectives. First, I am a woman who has been married for twenty-six years. I have walked the marriage talk for over a quarter of a century. I did not marry the perfect man, nor am I the perfect partner. But I have learned a few lessons along the way. When difficulty came, I found my way back to Truth—the Word of God. I have learned the necessity of a strong foundation. You will, too. I have also learned the importance of guarding my mind.

Second, I am a trained marriage and family therapist. I

have listened to hundreds of couples in distress over the past twenty years. Each story, although unique in its presentation, becomes strikingly familiar. In almost every case the problem could be traced to one source—either one or both spouses got out of alignment with God's way of thinking and doing things. As simple as this sounds, it is complex and not always easy to see.

Christian couples have an embarrassing record when it comes to divorce. According to Barna Research Group Online:

- One out of four adults (25 percent) has been divorced (1999).

- The divorce rate among both Christians and non-Christians has remained stable across the past half decade (1999).

- Born-again Christians are slightly more likely than non-Christians to go through a divorce, with 26 percent of born-agains and 22 percent of non-Christians having gone through a divorce at some time in their life (1999).[1]

These data are disturbing, especially when you consider Christians have access to the transforming power of the gospel. Obviously, we can choose to use that power, ignore it or take advantage of it only when it's convenient. When we are not plugged in to God's life-changing power, the culture seduces us by disguising truth or rendering it relative. Without Truth, transformation, whether individual or relational, is unlikely.

Lies are the ageless strategy of seduction. After all, it was a lie that led Eve to taste the forbidden fruit. She believed a falsehood and then acted on that belief. The result was estrangement from God followed by broken relationship.

If you want to prevent divorce, use this book to help you

identify the lies that creep into your thinking and slowly erode your relationship. Then counter those lies with biblical truth and sound strategies to build a satisfying and happy marriage. Every chapter provides specific ways to do this.

If you worry about divorce, you need to read this book. Divorce isn't a train wreck waiting to happen. You don't have to be one of the gloomy statistics that say your turn is coming. In fact, you can be one of a growing multitude who prevents divorce by applying what you learn in this book.

If you are already divorced, then pay close attention. You don't want divorce to happen again. Learn from your mistakes, and move on with life. Don't do what I've seen too many times—unconsciously move into another marriage and hope things will be different. This is a set-up for failure. Three times is not a charm. Be proactive using the divorce-proofing strategies you will learn in this book.

If you are in the process of getting a divorce, there are things you can do to turn the situation around. During my twenty years as a marital therapist, I've seen couples on the brink of divorce reverse the damage and make their relationships work again. It's never too late or too hopeless. However, both of you must open your eyes to the truth. The Bible promises that the truth can set you free (John 8:32). This isn't hype or a false claim. Discover that truth, then make real changes—and make them now!

Think of divorce-proofing like a parent childproofing a house for a toddler. First you must identify the dangers, then learn strategies to make things safe. Finally, put into action what you know. It doesn't matter how much you worry, plan or obsess. If your thinking is off, your strategies will fail and your solutions won't work.

While I recognize that no marriage is beyond the *possibility* of divorce, you can be proactive. Divorce is preventable. Let's begin with ten lies that lead to divorce. Take a moment, reach for that cup of coffee (latte, espresso, cappuccino or whatever your beverage of choice), get comfortable and read on to see if you, like many, have allowed lies to pull you away, consciously or unconsciously, into dangerous waters. It's time to improve on the divorce statistics by divorce-proofing your marriage.

–LINDA S. MINTLE, PH.D.

CHAPTER 1

Lies, Lies and More Lies

Seduced

I think of my good friends both in and out of ministry who are counted in the divorce statistics. I flash back to the night I sat with one friend as she cried herself to sleep, still reeling from the announcement that her husband was leaving her for another woman. He seemed to take pleasure in hurting her with the news. Stunned by his revelation, she sank into despair. How could she have been so naive to trust a man who practiced deception?

"The affair," he explained, "just happened because I was unhappy. I found someone who understands me and is interested in the same things. You and I have grown apart. You'd be better off with someone who really cares for you."

As we cried together and talked, the woundings from my

friend's childhood became apparent. She had repeated the familiar pattern learned from her family of origin. Like her mother, she married a man who emotionally abused her but took no responsibility for the hurt. The pain was intense, all mixed up—dad, husband, men. There was so much to sort out, but the wound was too fresh. Somewhere in this mess, a lie began to grow.

I remembered the helplessness my husband and I felt when another friend's wife left him and then lied to the Christian community about the reasons for her leaving. Not only did he face incredible loss, but also the unfounded shame she publicly heaped upon him. As friends, we tried to talk about the lies, but we were rebuffed and told we were being abusive. As a therapist, I marveled at how easily she could take the words of an uninformed counselor and twist them to support her decision.

We knew this couple had experienced problems throughout their marriage, but nothing was so despairing that it couldn't be repaired or changed. They never took the time to work with a marital therapist and attack those problems. God's immeasurable grace was loudly pronounced for the act of divorce, but not for restoration. Why would she resort to this drastic step when there was so much that could be done with a very willing partner? I knew the answer—it had to do with deception.

I thought about my own twenty-six-year marriage, which is strong, but had its rocky moments in the beginning. I was young and heavily influenced by the reigning culture of feminism. "I am woman; hear me roar" was a euphemism for *watch me become self-absorbed*. As I filled my head with feminist protest, self-obsession and the self-fulfillment ideology of the 1970s, my thoughts and actions were not always pleasing to the Lord.

I was not prepared to take on the strength of the ideology

that flooded me in graduate school. At the time I didn't recognize the constant intellectual assault that was attacking my values. Sometimes the war for my mind was subtle. Other times it was a direct attack against God and everything I believed. And no one around me was addressing this threat. Instead I was blindsided by the power of me. The culture wanted to obviate God from my consciousness. In a confused state of self-definition, I allowed myself to buy into this line of thinking. I began to believe the lies of the culture.

I was told that I could make things happen on my own. I was in charge of my destiny. Fresh from the wound of my brother's death, I remembered the vow I made after seeing the depth of agony my sister-in-law endured trying to pick up the pieces of her shattered life—I would never be dependent on a man. God could sit in the backseat, but I was driving the car. God and men (my husband included) needed to understand a few things about feminine power.

When I finally realized feminism was a cover-up for the deeper fear of losing my husband through death, I started to change. Strengthening my relationship with the Lord through repentance and self-examination (thankfully I had not forgotten the foundation of my biblical training), I was taken aback at how easy it had been to get off base. I was raised in a Christian family, went to church, loved God and yet had become veiled by an enemy whose sole purpose is to deceive and destroy. He tried, unsuccessfully, to destroy me. If I allowed him to play on my fears, he could also destroy my marriage.

We are wounded through life by circumstances, people and our own stupidity. The enemy takes shots at us through those woundings. His purpose is to deceive us and, ultimately, to destroy us. Divorce is the *end* destruction of a holy union. It comes through believing lies.

For some reason, cultural lies seem easier to embrace than biblical truth. Who wants to do the hard work of forgiveness and reconciliation? Justification and compromise are hallmarks of our postmodern life. We find ourselves accommodating and tolerating; our thinking has been altered. It's no surprise, then, that our behavior follows.

Lies are all around us. They bombard us from the culture, but also from our family and those who influence us. Sometimes we create lies in order to twist and distort a situation, attempting to avoid responsibility or obedience. Lies lead to emotional reactions that lead to behavior. Break the lie, and feelings change. When feelings change, behavior changes. Perception is different. Perception influences thinking, and so the cycle goes.

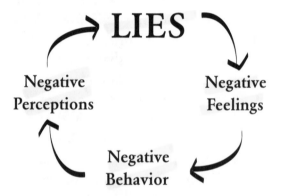

Here's the most damaging lie: We don't believe that the change needed to live peacefully and joyfully with our spouse is really possible. Oh, maybe we've seen a few testimonies of restored marriages on shows like *The 700 Club*. Still, we don't really believe that same transforming power is available for us. We buy the lie that our situation is too desperate, too angry or too hopeless.

Are you aware that Jesus constantly talked about unbelief as an obstacle to accessing His transforming power? Unbelief is still our worst enemy when it comes to changing the status quo, fighting habits or dealing with past woundings.

It's true that many couples need major repair work. And

in reality, you can only work on *you* unless you have a willing partner. I am acutely aware of the fact that many of you don't have a willing partner. Don't despair. There are still steps you can take.

For those of you doing the divorcing, I would encourage you to consider this. In all my years of practice, I have rarely seen anyone leave a marriage and go on to the next relationship without the same issues resurfacing on some level. Take my advice. Do everything you can to repair your current relationship. Divorce only delays the inevitable work.

Here's an example. A couple came in for marital counseling determined to divorce. Neither felt they could work through their differences. There was too much hurtful history, too many issues of trust and too much damage. I admit, they both had suffered greatly at the hand of the other, and the work to shape up their relationship would be major. But it was obvious to me that if they didn't make changes now, these same problems would resurface down the road.

I asked if they would give me eight weeks to identify their problems and provide strategies for change. From my experience, most divorcing couples are so busy blaming each other that they haven't clearly identified their own contribution to the problems. Usually this involves believing a lie. When they finally recognize and admit their part, change begins. Sometimes for the first time a couple will understand exactly *why* (the lie) they are doing *what* they are doing. Once the lie is identified, they are responsible to change. My job is to open their eyes and give them tools. But I can't make people do the work.

The couple I was counseling had a choice—address issues now with the current spouse, or do the work later with new players.

They declined my offer and divorced. Five years later, now married to new spouses, each one contacted me separately again. Both remembered my prediction and admitted the same problems were resurfacing in the new relationships. The original wife was on her third marriage, and jokingly said, "I guess on the third strike I'm out, so let's start dealing with my issues."

The husband, brought to therapy by his second wife, was surprised to hear her say, "I'm starting to realize why his first wife left him. I was pretty naive to think he wouldn't act the same with me." Finally! It was time to tackle the issues. Each regretted not doing this earlier with their original spouses.

It's a rare person who comes to my office and says, "I'm having marital problems. Let's talk about what I'm doing to make matters worse." More often I get the very well-played blame game—it is the fault of my spouse, my job, my in-laws, too much stress . . . (add your favorite here, the list is long).

The typical complaint is, "I can't, because she/he does . . . " Here are some variations on that theme. "I married a jerk." This may be true, but guess what? You chose that jerk. "He wasn't a jerk when I married him. He turned jerky (not related to beef) later." Nice idea, but not likely. You may not have recognized the "jerkiness" prior to marriage, but it was there, brewing under the surface. "I was unconscious when I took my vows. Now I'm awake, and this marriage is a nightmare!" Sorry, you are still responsible for that unconscious choice. Getting out is not the solution.

Speaking of nightmares, some of you thought you could change him or her for the better. You know . . . "He'll stop drinking because he loves me." "It doesn't matter that his dad is a serial killer." "She'll settle down when she has kids." "When he gets out of prison, he'll be a changed man." The truth? The likelihood of you changing your partner significantly is about the same as me winning the lottery (which is pretty low considering I don't even play it!).

Here's another misconception: Marital mending depends on the razzle-dazzle of a good therapist. I'm pretty good at razzle-dazzle, but that alone won't divorce-proof your marriage. Instead, your marriage depends on how willing you are to do what you need to do to be accountable for your thoughts and actions.

When trouble erupts, many of you go to therapy. Good step, but you must also *want* to reconcile. Be honest—there are other motives, ones that inexperienced therapists sometimes fall for. You want to ease your conscience. You want someone to "feel" your pain. You want to say you made the effort. You want to prove how bad your partner is (people are very good at this one). The last thing you want is someone like me in your face telling you that no marriage is beyond saving.

If you want it fixed, it can get fixed. Other than the three biggies—abuse, abandonment and unrepentant infidelity (and even these aren't beyond hope)—marriages that end up on the therapist's couch can be restored. But you have to want it to happen.

I went to a marital conference a few years ago presented by someone whom I greatly admire. She is well known in the field of marriage and family therapy. Her work was influential in my training, so I expected two days of new insight. It was new all right, but hardly insightful.

She started the conference by saying that marriage is only a relationship, not something we should be tied to "until death do us part." "Marriage is an extremely fragile relationship," she asserted. "It's unreasonable to expect people to stay together. Basically, we need to rethink the 'myth' of marriage. Perhaps it's outdated to expect two people to love only each other for a lifetime. Maybe we should redefine marriage to make it fit reality. The reality is . . . divorce is likely."

At the break I compared notes with several colleagues, including two chaplains. To my total dismay, not one of them was bothered by her remarks. The consensus among the group was, "Most of us are divorced, so why not just change the expectation and reduce the guilt. We'll all be better off."

The secular view is that divorce happens, will continue to happen, and there is little you can do about it. But divorce needn't be a painful, ever-present reality. "Till death do us part" is an attainable goal. Don't believe marriage is a "myth" in need of redefinition.

Most of us don't live as transformed creations; we still struggle with family problems, rebellion, compromise, self-centeredness and other issues related to distorted thoughts. We govern our lives by feelings. We sin; we give in. We want things our way, and we struggle through life because we refuse to live life God's way. We have our own system, and we are pretty committed to it—even when it doesn't work. Our way of doing things is what we know—what is comfortable, even if it's not right.

No one is completely immune from divorce because deception is all around us. And you don't have control over another person. There are times when people must walk away from a relationship because of real or potential harm. But I do know that in most cases, divorce is preventable, particularly for Christians. Prevention starts by recognizing the lies.

We break covenant just as we break speeding laws. It's dangerous, but we'll take our chances. "Yes, the children suffer, but they'll adjust. My momentary happiness is of utmost importance." We get so caught up in our relationship needs that we forget our true purpose in life. We are not here to be happy all the time. Jesus did not call us to self-gratification. Yes, it's helpful to know yourself and get your needs met, but knowing God is far more important. Knowing God is supposed to make a difference in our relationships. His system is very different from the larger culture, but we have to know it and be willing to embrace it.

Transform your marriage into something satisfying and godly. Begin by asking, "Do I meet the three preconditions necessary to divorce-proof my marriage?"

CHAPTER 2

Three Key Preconditions to Divorce-Proofing

Ready, Set, Go

Before we launch into ten lies that lead to divorce, review these three preconditions to divorce-proofing your marriage:

1. Consider the Possibility That You Contribute to Ongoing or Past Problems

I know, it's tough to admit. But a marital couple is composed of two people who bring unique issues to the relationship. Before you complain about what your partner is or is not doing, first take a hard look at yourself.

I am not asking you to be the scapegoat for problems or to be responsible for things that are not yours. I am asking you to entertain the idea that you are not the perfect mate. You may be close to perfection, far away from perfection or somewhere in between, so can we open up to this possibility? Start by asking these questions:

- Do I carry old wounds from my past?

- Am I operating out of fear or other unhealthy emotions?

- Have I blamed my spouse for things that are really mine?

- Am I allowing myself to be deceived, falling away from the truth?

- Am I willing to believe change is possible?

- Am I walking in a close and intimate relationship with God, or have I relegated Him to a backseat position?

- Do I even believe what God says is true?

When you allow deception to creep into your life—a little here, a little there—soon you deviate from God's plan and become the enemy's pawn. The further you veer from God's truth, the more difficult it is to keep the marital covenant.

It's time to stop blaming and to assess accurately your contribution to the damage. Beginning to do this opens the possibility for change. Start by asking God to reveal things in your life that need changing. These things may be unrelated to your spouse, but they will certainly affect him or her. Spend time in prayer, and listen for God to speak.

2. Recognize That You Don't Have Control Over Your Spouse's Will, But You Do Have a Great Deal of Influence

The second precondition to divorce-proofing your marriage

is recognizing the influence you have with your spouse. Maybe you don't feel influential, but you are. There is a well-known physics axiom that states, "For every action, there is an equal and opposite reaction." Apply this reality to your relationship.

For every action in marriage, there is a spousal reaction, sometimes equal, sometimes opposite. You can only control *your* actions, regardless of how your partner behaves. No matter how bad things get, you can exercise self-control. Self-control is a desired quality—one that is not reinforced much in our culture. God promises us self-control:

> **But the fruit of the Spirit is love, joy, peace, long-suffering, kindness, goodness, faithfulness, gentleness, self-control.**
>
> —GALATIANS 5:22–23

According to this verse, love is the fruit. All fruit grows from a seed. The seed is the Word of God. You plant the seed (the Word) in your heart first. The result of knowing and believing God's Word is love. Said another way, the result of planting the seed is growing a crop of fruit (love). God's love, then, produces self-control.

When you work to develop self-control, you concentrate far less on what your partner is doing and more on your own actions and reactions. A change in one person creates a change in another. It's like a dance.

I've borrowed the dance metaphor from author Harriet Lerner's book *Dance of Anger*.[1] I will refer to it in more depth in chapter 5. The idea is this. Imagine yourself dancing with your spouse. (If you are too angry or this is too much of a leap, just imagine two people dancing.) You make a move, and your partner follows. This interaction continues. One motion follows another. Taken together, these motions create the choreography of the dance.

Couples create dances together. One spouse behaves one way, the other follows with a behavior. These actions repeat and follow a pattern. Over time, couples lock into familiar dances. Some dances are very well known because they were rehearsed growing up with your first family. Other dances are learned with your partner and practiced over and over.

Some dances can be wonderful, romantic, dreamy, soothing, supportive, easy, flowing, creative, innovative and fluid. Other dances can be jerky, tense, toe crushing, out of step, body slamming and embarrassing. Obviously the latter are the dances we don't like and need to change.

How do you change the dance? By changing *your* step in the dance. You can't force your partner to move differently. Some spouses will make a new move based on suggestion or helpful feedback. Others will not. But *you* can take a different step. When you do, the result will likely be tension. Either you will fall back into the old step, or your spouse will accommodate the new. If you don't give in, the dance has to change. It feels awkward at first, tense and terribly uncomfortable, but eventually the steps begin to form a new pattern, a new dance. Here's your hope: By changing your step in the dance, the dance will change if you don't go back to the old way.

Notice I didn't say your actions/reactions *determine* your partner's actions. I said they *influence*. But when you firmly practice a new step, you have more influence than you realize. Most of us feel the tension of taking a new step, and consequently, we give in to the old familiar way. It's easier and less exhausting, but it results in the same old dance. Nothing much changes.

Your partner has a free will and can choose to exercise it for the good of the relationship or toward its destruction. That's the scary part of relationships—we join in a holy union with someone over whom we don't have ultimate control. But think about the dance again. We have control over *our* steps, which influence the entire movement. Our steps count because they create the dance.

When one person in a couple decides to walk away from the things of God and step into the world's system, trouble begins. You can't force someone to turn back to God. Sound familiar? You may have screamed, cried, manipulated, been hurtful, angry, pitiful, depressed, anxious, perfect, tolerant, condemning, distant, dependent or dragged your spouse to counseling (add whatever else I've missed here). Yet nothing has changed—your spouse is still bent on divorcing you. It seems you've tried every new step in the dance imaginable.

If so, then your problem is probably a spiritual one. Your spouse has hardened his or her heart to the things of God. Nothing will move that spouse because he or she is determined to pursue a new dance without you. Your spouse no longer wants you as a dance partner. He or she thinks there is a more talented dancer out there. The truth is that the coveted new dance will hardly be new—your spouse will merely choose a new partner.

Your hope in these situations is that your spouse will be convicted of sin and awaken from spiritual slumber to have a true encounter with the living God. Pray to that end, and make sure you read chapter 12.

3. You Must Become Aware of the Spiritual Deception Along the Road to Divorce

We forget that marriage is a *holy* act. The dividing of two people through divorce is an attempt to sever the union of spirits. Divorce doesn't absolve that union—it simply separates the partners physically. It only takes one person to sever the tie, but a host of people are deeply affected for the rest of their lives.

To be willing to dissolve a holy tie, you must be deceived. The deception process is slow and insidious. It begins with a little disappointment, unhappiness or wounding. You entertain the notion that someone or something else can make up the difference or provide something you don't have. It's the same lie that Eve bought in the garden.

Remember Eve? She could have any tree in the garden from which to eat except one. That's the one Satan used to lure her. When he appeared in the form of a lowly snake, she listened to his ideas. Satan lied to her: "You can eat it and you won't die." We might all be running around a Middle Eastern paradise naked if she had replied, "Satan, you liar, take a crawl. I know what God said."

Take this position with even the smallest thing that goes against God. When God's Word is clear on something, don't believe anything else. Eve ate the fruit and found out God was serious about His Word. Today, everyone who eats the forbidden fruit of divorce lives with the consequences of that choice. Certainly God still loves them and shows His grace and mercy. But natural consequences follow our actions.

You may be in the middle of very difficult circumstances with a spouse. You may even be separated. Let me say a few words about separation. At times, marital separation is warranted to stop abusive behavior or to show that you mean business when dealing with unrepented sinful behavior. Separation might be a step toward reconciliation. It can be a strategy used to say, "Knock it off. Get serious, get control, and stop misbehaving. When you can show me that you are a changed person (over time), we'll reunite."

With couples who are so busy blaming each other and so toxic in their interactions, separation can temporarily stop the negativity. The purpose of separation is to help individual spouses think more clearly about the relationship and work on personal issues. Time committed to prayer is essential.

Prayer is directed at asking God to reveal your part in the problem, not to seek His will about divorce. You already know His will is to reconcile. He told you so in His Word.

Counseling is highly recommended during separation so that change can be monitored. And notice I said "over time"—a condition that proves the trustworthiness of change. Separation works when confession ends in repentance (a true turning of behavior) and a commitment to change is made.

Separation doesn't work when a spouse has already determined to get out of the marriage and uses the separation to do as he or she pleases. It also doesn't work if a spouse refuses to address the spiritual, behavioral or emotional issues of the marriage. In these cases the spouse has already disconnected emotionally. Separation only reinforces that distance.

For the Christian, reconciliation should always be the goal. Reconciliation requires forgiveness and a true change of heart. One or both spouses may have to make serious behavior changes. However, change usually begins with a willful decision to think and behave differently. Add God's power to the mix, and reconciliation is possible. I speak from professional experience.

Over the years of counseling couples, I can only think of a few times when I felt a marriage was truly not salvageable. And then, I regret to say my position was probably due to a lack of faith. I wasn't sure that even God could pull these marriages out of the fire. Of course He could have if the spouses had willing hearts and if they had submitted to His way. But God doesn't knock people over the head and demand they behave His way. He gave us free will. We have to *choose* to reconcile.

Many couples don't make this choice. I have had the following conversation with these couples: "I know you have little if any feelings left for your spouse. I know much has happened to damage trust severely. I know there are deep wounds, and it looks impossible to reconcile. But are you *willing* to try? Can we try to find a way to reconcile this relationship? I know you can't see any of this now, so it would require stepping out in faith."

I can still see the faces of those who looked me straight in the eyes and replied, "No, I'm not willing."

There's not much that can be done at that point. That is a flat-out rejection of any possibility for reconciliation. Spiritually, such a response throws God out of the picture. In effect, you are saying, "I don't want to . . . even if God can." The lack of "want to" can be based on a number of factors—too tired, hurt, distant, don't care, pride and other factors. But it boils down to this: You've given up.

God sent Jesus to make a way where there was no way. Don't reject His love and sacrifice. Don't reject His grace. What He did was enough. Don't limit His possibilities. Try.

Don't be another casualty of divorce, no matter how desperate things look. Be an example, a testimony of God's grace and transformation. Learn how to divorce-proof your marriage by stopping the lies that lead to divorce. Discover the truths that can save your marriage.

If you are already divorced, resolve all the issues around your divorce. I can't overstate the importance of doing this work. Not only will you be healthier in future relationships, but you will help others avoid a similar path. If you do the work, you'll have much to offer others.

Do you want to stop divorce? Do you believe it's possible to have a marriage in which divorce is never an option? Do you want to understand how we get off the marital path? If you do, read on. You'll learn how to divorce-proof your marriage. You will learn how you and your spouse can determine the outcome of your relationship.

Three Key Preconditions to Divorce-Proofing

He will completely fool those who are on their way
to hell because they have said "no" to the Truth;
they have refused to believe it and love it, and let
it save them, *so God will allow them to believe lies with
all their hearts,* and all of them will be justly judged
for believing falsehood, refusing the Truth, and
enjoying their sins.

–2 Thessalonians 2:10–12, tlb, emphasis added

CHAPTER 3

Escape and Avoidance

Lie #1

Marriage is a contract.

I looked at the attractive couple sitting on opposite ends of my therapy couch. Facing outward, one stared at the picture on the wall and the other, out the window. The uncomfortable silence mirrored their relationship. Neither made eye contact.

It's Just Not Working—Tom and Rachel

Tom and Rachel referred themselves for marital therapy. Both admitted they really didn't want to see me but felt obligated to give therapy a try. I suggested they start by trying to look at one another and say something. Rachel rolled her eyes. Her voice was angry as she asked, "If we could talk to each other, do you think we would be here?"

"No," I calmly replied, "but that's the point of therapy–to

get you to do things you aren't already doing."

With another look of disgust, Rachel decided to give me the *necessary background.* "I married Tom shortly after we both graduated from college. Tom was the kind of man I thought would make a good husband—ambitious, affectionate, conversational and family minded. Obviously I was wrong," she underlined. Tom sat motionless.

Fresh out of college they were eager to make money and establish their respective careers. What they didn't expect was the price they would pay for success. Rachel secured an entry-level position at a high-powered accounting firm. The opportunity for advancement presented itself if she was willing to put in long hours. Tom landed a job as a sales representative for a growing media company. His job required constant travel. Work was all consuming. By the end of the day with their energy spent, both collapsed in bed. Surely this exhausting schedule would relent. Five years later not much had changed, except that Tom and Rachel felt like strangers who occasionally had dinner together. She was angry, and he was distant.

Tom sat quietly on the couch as Rachel recalled another story of her needs gone unmet. He rarely responded to any of Rachel's mounting complaints. *Rachel has changed,* he thought to himself. *She agreed to the plan for financial security, and now all she does is complain.* He wasn't getting the support he needed from her. Didn't she understand that he didn't like being away from home either? But hadn't they agreed to put up with the inconveniences until they reached their goals?

Tom was tired—physically and emotionally. This marriage wasn't working out the way he expected. Maybe marriage should have waited until they were better established in their careers. He couldn't understand why Rachel was so unhappy. They were just doing what they imagined. Why was Rachel so angry with him all the time? He didn't like her constant irritation, so he withdrew.

Escape and Avoidance

Intuitively Rachel sensed Tom's distance. He was so attentive when they were dating, but now she rarely saw him. Why didn't he care that the marriage was falling apart? He seemed so cold. He rarely talked anymore. She couldn't live with a man whose work commanded all his affection. This wasn't what she had bargained for in a marriage.

The silence continued. Tom looked back out the window. Rachel drew a deep sigh and stared at the wall. *It wasn't what they expected. Their needs weren't met.* On those two points they completely agreed. They asked if I thought a separation might help. Call me slow, but I thought that was one of the problems—too much time away from each other. Sighs of dejection escaped their lips.

They glanced at each other without my prompting and gave an all-knowing nod. Sitting forward on the couch with renewed energy, Rachel spoke. "We think we need to divorce. Our needs aren't getting met. We think it's time to call it quits."

Tom added, "We're still young. We haven't started a family yet. We realize we're not satisfying each other. Let's cut our losses and move on with our lives. I negotiate contracts with clients all the time. When our gains no longer outweigh our losses, we break the deal. This marital contract just isn't working out; that's how we see it. Before we get too much farther into this relationship and have kids, we need to make a clean break now."

Tom and Rachel's view of marriage is consistent with most American couples. They stay married as long as their needs are being met. They believe in something called *social exchange theory*—you should *get* more than you *give*. Marriage is seen as a relationship involving costs and rewards. You get rewards, but you must also give up something for those rewards. When the costs outweigh the rewards, it may be time to break the contract.

Marriage *is* a contract, legally speaking. According to the dictionary, a *contract* is an agreement between two people, enforceable by law, to do a specific thing. The formal agreement of marriage fits that definition. Divorce is the breaking of that legal contract. If you believe this, you are not totally off base. You're just missing the bigger picture and are operating under the popular view of marriage, not God's view.

Tom and Rachel are dissatisfied people preoccupied with what they are not getting from each other. This is not a case of desertion, abuse or adultery. It's two people who built their marriage on the wrong foundation. Add stress, and the foundation begins to crack. Add intense ongoing stress, and the foundation crumbles.

Truth #1

Marriage is a covenant designed by God.

What Tom and Rachel need to understand is that marriage is more than a contract. It was God's idea long before legal arrangements were added. God defines marriage as a *covenant*. Covenant is not based on the *quid pro quo* system of social exchange (you should get more than you give). Covenant is based on unconditional love—love that is an unbreakable promise between two parties. Understanding the difference between contract and covenant is a key to preventing divorce. Obviously, Tom and Rachel didn't have this understanding.

Escape and Avoidance

Contract vs. Covenant

Covenants were invented by God and thus are sacred. God made a covenant with His creation. He promised Adam and Eve to provide for all their needs in the Garden of Eden. The only restriction was that they could not touch one specific tree. Adam and Eve's choice to disobey resulted in expulsion from the place of perfect provision.

Then God promised another provision, one that would forever eradicate their sin—the coming of the Messiah (Gen. 3:14–21). Adam and Eve's sin didn't cancel God's plan, but their responses certainly changed things. Like the first couple, we can choose to do things our way or God's way. Most of us stubbornly choose our own way.

God also established a covenant with Noah. He promised to save Noah, his family and nonhuman creatures from destruction. When God destroyed every other living creature on the earth by a flood, He kept His promise to Noah. God didn't say to Noah, "Here's a plan. If you work hard enough and I am satisfied, I'll follow through with My promise. You have one hundred years; get started." Instead God made an offer to spare Noah. The covenant was not dependent on Noah's response. God extended His hand regardless of Noah's choice. However, the potential blessings of the covenant were related to how Noah behaved. And in order to be saved, Noah had to act on God's unbreakable promise.

Perhaps the best-known example of Old Testament covenant was the one God established with Abraham. (See Genesis 15.) He promised to make a mighty nation from Abraham's descendants and to give him the land of Canaan. The promise was given before Abraham had children. It required that Abraham agree and believe by faith. Like Noah, the covenant was unconditional, but the blessings were determined by Abraham's response—a blameless and faithful walk before God.

Abraham's wife, Sarah, was old and beyond childbearing

years. The promise to have many descendents was an impossible feat in the natural. But Abraham had faith. He believed what God said even when he could see no immediate evidence of it happening. His faith allowed God to work a miracle.

Finally God sent Jesus as the ultimate expression of His unconditional love for us. Jesus was treated poorly, to say the least. Yet nothing people did to Him (and you know how badly He was treated) resulted in His breaking the covenant. He could have bailed out and gone back to heaven because of the rejection. He had every "right" to call off the arrangement. But He didn't because He and the Father made a promise. He loves us just because we are His creation. And because He loves us, He kept His covenant. He came to earth, died a horrible death and rose again to provide us a way out of our sin. As Christians, we are covered by His blood covenant, and nothing can change that.

Marital Covenant

Being *in covenant* means you are unconditionally committed to someone. When God made a covenant with us through Christ, He made a commitment never to leave us. Of course, He wants that commitment to be mutual and reciprocal. But because of free will, that part is up to us.

What can we learn from biblical covenants that will apply to our relationships today? Well, God's way is to extend a promise and never break it, a promise based on unconditional love. Loving someone doesn't depend on what they do *for you*, nor should it depend on how they respond. Perhaps our closest experience with unconditional love is the love we have for our children. They disappoint us and do wrong things, but we love them anyway. That's how God wants us to be with each other—loving each other just because He loves us.

A covenantal relationship also requires we extend forgiveness to each other. As He hung on a cross in agony and pain, Jesus, beaten, mocked and rejected, cried out to the Father to forgive His torturers. He didn't wait to be justified, and His forgiveness wasn't dependent on them coming forward to confess their offense. What an example of forgiveness! Because He forgives us, we are to forgive each other, extending His grace.

Christ exemplified compassion and empowerment. He was moved with compassion; He healed, but then He challenged those He met to walk in His way. His mission was to prepare and strengthen His followers to take on the challenges of the day. As His followers, we too should be building esteem, encouraging and strengthening each other to accomplish all we're intended to be.

God introduced His plan for marriage in Genesis and repeated it in the Gospels. Marriage was designed as a covenant, modeled after God's relationship with us. Marriage is a vow of commitment made to God and your partner for life. When marriage is reduced to conditions—based on give and get as Tom and Rachel did—you've strayed from God's way of doing things.

So what does it mean to have a covenant marriage? It means divorce isn't an option. I know what you are thinking—*Get real! Easy for her to say…she hasn't lived in my marriage. I'm in an impossible position. Besides, look at the high divorce rate.* The covenantal view has nothing to do with how difficult anyone's marriage is. God fashioned marriage, and it's still His model today—no matter how impossible it seems in the new millennium. The issue then is to obey—not complain that it can't be accomplished or decide the model is outdated.

Would things be different if you believed you always had to work things out in your marriage? Would you try harder? Would you base your actions on your feelings? Would you look outside the marriage for a better deal? Extend forgiveness more often? Deal with anger faster? Stop avoiding conflict?

Would you try to love your mother-in-law? How about focusing more on the positive attributes of your partner, trying to build up your partner rather than finding fault? The answers to these questions depend on what you believe to be true about relationships. If, in the back of your mind, you believe you can get out of the arrangement, the exit door is always open. This thinking affects your behavior.

If you agree that marriage is a covenant, then what should you do if you're stuck in an unhappy relationship? You may believe that it would take a miracle to make your relationship work. Could be, but miracles still happen! This may sound trite but true—*Pray for restoration*. Pray diligently without ceasing. Don't faint or grow weary. God is the God of the impossible. I know this sounds like Christian rhetoric, but it's based on the character and goodness of God. Restoration of your marriage is possible—just as it was for Dan and Susan.

Pray for Restoration

Dan and Susan were unhappy for years. They had been to marital counseling many times, resolved nothing and now only felt contempt for one another. By all accounts (my own included), the outcome looked bleak. Divorce was always on their minds. Even though neither felt anything for the other, they agreed to do one thing—pray and fast for a period of time. I asked them to separate and concentrate their spare time on prayer and seeking the Lord for guidance. Since they had been married sixteen years, I hoped they would at least give God a few weeks of undivided attention.

They agreed. Separately they fasted and prayed. I asked them if they felt God released them to divorce. Neither felt a release. I wasn't surprised considering God would not direct them to do something against His own Word. But they needed a miracle to restore them to a place of love and commitment.

I asked each of them to write down all the offenses they

felt had been committed over the past sixteen years of marriage. This took a few weeks. The lists were long and detailed. Then, I asked them to pray over every item and choose to forgive each offense until the list was completed. I reminded them that because God forgave them, they too needed to extend this same forgiveness to each other.

Next I assigned them to make a second list of good points, happy times or positive events that took place over sixteen years of marriage. They were surprised themselves at how long those lists grew. They exchanged lists and went back to prayer, thanking God for each memory. Those positive qualities and events had been lost in the fog of marital unhappiness.

Finally they were to pray for a miracle of restored love, by faith believing it could happen. It has been my experience that most Christian couples who divorce are unwilling to believe for restoration. They don't desire *restoration*—they *want out*. They reject the possibility that God can work a miracle in them because they've seen no evidence. Unbelief sets in—*What if God can't do this? What if nothing changes? Why did God allow this to happen in the first place? Why hasn't He changed things?*

You serve a powerful God. He is able to do exceedingly, abundantly above all you ask or think (Eph. 3:20). But you must ask Him and believe for a miracle. If He can heal cancer, remove tumors and save family members, He can restore marriages. Remind yourself what God has done and what He is capable of doing. Have faith. Miracles of marriage restoration happen to those who believe. (See Truth #10.)

Don't Keep Wondering About Your Covenant

Another problem related to keeping covenant is wondering if you married the "right" person. Stop wondering—because you already did the deed. It does no good to keep begging the question.

Maybe you married for the wrong reasons—you wanted out of the house; you were pregnant; you were afraid of being alone; you were on the rebound; you wanted to rescue someone; you felt pressured; you needed someone to re-parent you. Not a great reason to marry in the bunch, but this is not the time to recriminate. It's time to work *through* your mistake and correct whatever motivated the original decision.

Rhonda married Mike because she was pregnant. Within two years, she regretted her decision. Mike was not the kind of man she really wanted for a lifetime partner. He was too quiet, too boring and unsure of himself. Rhonda began to complain about her husband. Her friends said maybe she should divorce him since she only married him to give the baby a father. But Rhonda and Mike were Christians. I asked her to stop focusing on what Mike *wasn't* and to focus instead on why she got pregnant. What motivated her to have unprotected premarital sex? Had she worked on those issues? Was she trying to grow? And had she shared her concerns with Mike? The answer was no to each question.

When I talked with Mike, he had similar concerns. He married Rhonda out of obligation, but felt she was a bit too extroverted for him. He was more comfortable with a quieter type—a woman who wanted to be a mom above all else. Mike had made no effort to look at his premarital behavior.

The two started exploring the reasons behind their promiscuity. Rhonda thought getting close to men meant having sex. Mike's lack of boundaries with Rhonda had to do with major insecurity. Once we started addressing Rhonda's intimacy issues and Mike's insecurities in therapy, the couple had more respect for one another. They were also growing together emotionally. Mike came out of his shell and was more fun to be around. Rhonda relaxed when she realized that love was about more than sex.

The two had never asked each other for forgiveness for

their premarital behavior. They had repented to God—but not to each other. When they did, something happened in the spiritual dimension. There was a release of anger and hurt.

The final step was to pray that God would help them honor the covenant they had made before Him. If each stayed willing to continue working on past and present issues, remained honest and asked God to change them into models of Christlikeness, there was hope for a long-lasting relationship.

Years have passed, and Rhonda and Mike are still together. But they've stopped wondering about their decision to marry. Instead, they've relied on God to help them honor that decision and transform them into God's best.

Stuck in a Bad Marriage

If you feel "stuck" in your marriage because you made a bad choice, married unconsciously or had a lapse of stupidity, there is still hope for a better day. It is possible to have a good marriage even when it starts off wrong, goes wrong or just feels wrong. How so? Start with foundational belief—marriage is a *covenant*, not a *contract*. Then read the rest of this book! I'll say it again—most marriages are salvageable. Even when problems don't seem solvable, people stay together. You may be surprised to learn that solving problems is not the basis for a happy, satisfied marriage.

Am I saying there are no conditions under which divorce is permissible? No, of course not. I've been a therapist far too long to be that naive. There are biblical conditions under which divorce is permitted. But most divorces are pursued because of personal unhappiness, selfishness and an unwillingness to extend grace and forgiveness. Most divorces are about hurting back or refusing to be hurt again.

Jesus addressed the difficulty of keeping the marital vow when the Pharisees questioned Him about the Law of Moses permitting divorce (Matt. 19:3, 7). Jesus reminded them that divorce was a concession only to the "hardness of your heart" (Mark 10:3–5). Hardness of heart can lead to abuse, abandonment and repeated infidelity. These may be conditions under which separation and eventually divorce occur. If you are someone who has suffered domestic violence, repeated affairs and abandonment by a spouse, this is not meant to condemn or judge you. Obviously, there is biblical permission to address these conditions through divorce. No one wants you harmed or suffering. You are not the subject of this book.

I'm talking to people who simply want out for reasons other than abuse and repeated infidelity. Frankly, I've seen marriages turned around dramatically even under those conditions. The major marital complaint I hear most often is, "I'm just not happy" (related to Lie #6). OK, get happy, but don't use divorce as the solution. Unhappiness is often related to something in *you* rather than in the *other person*.

So begin by changing the way you think about marriage. If you are looking for a legal out, you'll probably find one. If instead you are looking for reconciliation and forgiveness, you will stay together under even the most difficult circumstances.

We have been taught to value personal happiness over all else. But when the moment of happiness passes, we still have to deal with the consequences of our choices. Value covenant. Learn to love what and how God loves, and you will find joy.

When the Contract Fails—John and Ann

Consider John and Ann, both Christians. Both are unhappy, but one has decided marriage is contractual. He wants out, claiming he no longer loves his wife. He flirts with other women and enjoys their responsiveness, something he says is lacking from his wife.

All John knows is that he no longer wants to be with Ann.

Escape and Avoidance

He has checked out emotionally. Why? He falsely believes another woman will make him happier. He has decided his wife is the source of all his unhappiness (which, by the way, is ridiculous—see Lie #4). He's bought the lie of contract—he's not getting what he wants, so he'll find another partner to give him what he needs. Nowhere in the discussion is there a concern for the long-term commitment he made to his wife. "For better or for worse" was only a cliché. "Stay and work it out" is nothing he wants to entertain.

John and Ann represent hundreds of couples who come to therapy. When I challenge them on the issue of covenant, they don't want to embrace it. Why? Because it means escape is not a solution. If John and Ann choose a Christian therapist, one of three things will happen:

1 John will work on his personal unhappiness and honor his commitment. He will inevitably learn that Ann is not the source of all his unhappiness.

2 John will be extremely uncomfortable with someone like me telling him to honor his covenant. He may drop out of therapy and do what he pleases. He'll tell others he tried therapy and it didn't work.

3 John will continue to believe marriage is a contract. It fits his desire to divorce, and he will.

When you decide to end a relationship, you behave differently. "Knowing" you can get out whenever things get rough changes everything. It is easier to take offense and keep it. It's easier not to try. It's easier to look elsewhere for need gratification. It's easier to be disappointed. It's easier to justify behavior, give up and focus on what you are not getting. It's easier to blame the other person. In fact, you're almost forced to do all the above in order to reinforce your obsession to leave.

There is a movement under way to bring back the idea of

covenant in American marriages. In 1997 politicians in the state of Louisiana adopted the first covenant marriage laws. Couples voluntarily and legally agree to receive premarital counseling and not to divorce unless adultery, abuse or abandonment has occurred. For couples considering divorce, a two-year waiting period with counseling is mandated. The intent of this law is to encourage couples to do everything possible for reconciliation—a novel idea in our culture of divorce. However, last year sixteen of seventeen states considering covenant marriage laws turned them down. In Louisiana, only 3 percent of newly married couples have chosen this option since the law was conceived.[1]

The church has finally begun to speak up. Family-focused ministries, counselors and conferences have mobilized resources to help people affirm their vows. But if you don't believe marriage is a covenant, no marriage encounter, enrichment or seminar you attend will matter. Everything will fall on deaf ears. Ever wonder why we have such a high rate of divorce despite all this available help? You may have the best intentions, but you end up like Don and Renee.

Don and Renee

Don and Renee did all the right things prior to marriage. They knew each other for two years, dated one year and were engaged for eight months. By the time the wedding came around, they knew each other well. They attended premarital courses at the local clinic and met with their pastor on a regular basis. Don's parents were married thirty years. They had their moments of conflict, but Don never doubted their love and commitment to one another. Don was confident he could give such a commitment to Renee.

Renee was more hesitant. Her parents divorced after twenty years of marriage, stating irreconcilable differences. As a teenager at the time of their divorce, Renee never knew what "irreconcilable differences" her parents had. They didn't fight. Renee's friend told her that "irreconcilable differences" was the standard line parents used to keep you out of their business and to end a marriage. But the not knowing bothered Renee. It made her question her own ability to stay in a lifelong commitment.

Renee mentioned her concern to Don. He understood her fear, which was based on her parents' divorce. He assured her that she wasn't doomed to repeat their pattern. Renee wasn't so sure. She recalled her past relationships with boyfriends. Every time she ran up against a major conflict, she left. She thought about the ache in her heart when her father moved out, and she was determined not to experience rejection from a man again. It hurt too much. So, she would be the one to leave when things got bad. She worried about her fear of rejection, but she felt too ashamed to tell anyone. After all, she finally had a man who loved her.

Over the next few years, Don and Renee endured the typical marital adjustments. When they argued, Renee would threaten to leave. Don asked her repeatedly not to say such a thing. They were supposed to be committed to each other. Why would she throw such a threat in his face? Maybe she needed to talk to someone who could help her deal with her fear.

Renee swore she wouldn't threaten to leave again, but in the middle of an argument the words poured out. She felt powerful as she said them, and she also didn't mind noticing the hurt in Don's eyes. Her past kept invading her thoughts. *No man will hurt me like my dad did when he walked away. I won't be left. I'll do the leaving first, even if I hurt Don. I don't ever want to feel that kind of pain again.*

Arguments became more frequent. Renee would threaten divorce and actually leave the house for hours. While away, she would tell herself how wrong it was to walk out: *I'm just like my father.* Maybe she really couldn't work out differences.

Maybe a lifelong commitment for her was simply a fairy tale.

So she talked to her friends. One divorced friend told her, "You can never really know what someone is like until you live with him. Now that you are married, you are seeing Don's true colors. Maybe you don't like what you see. No man is worth constant upset. Now maybe you understand better why I am divorced. Who can live with someone who argues all the time? You shouldn't give any man that kind of power over your life. Maybe you should separate for awhile."

Separation appealed to Renee. It would give her time to think. She could conquer the fear of being left if she just had time away from Don. But she was still too embarrassed to tell anyone about her fear. Wasn't it crazy for a twenty-eight-year-old woman to react to something that happened years ago? Instead of dealing with her fear, she began to question her beliefs about marriage. Marriage between two good people doesn't always work—that's what her friend told her. She began to believe a lie, rationalizing that she hadn't really been ready to marry anyone with this fear of rejection.

Don and Renee did separate, but they agreed to meet for marital therapy. Her friend recommended the therapist. Don didn't understand what was troubling his wife, but he was sure it could be worked out. After all, their marriage was a covenant.

The therapist turned to Renee and asked if she shared Don's view of covenant. "Not really," she replied. "I've never seen it work with anyone in my family. I come from a long line of divorce. I hoped I could be different, but that was naive. It's unrealistic to expect two people to stay together for life. Don't get me wrong. It's a great fantasy." The lie was now firmly implanted.

From that point on it was clear, Don had a different view. Sadly, Renee chose to avoid her fear and to embrace the lie that honoring her marital covenant was impossible. She did not reinforce her thinking with God's Word. Instead, she talked only with those who told her what she wanted to hear and played on her fears. Consequently Renee and Don divorced, without ever addressing Renee's fears or biblically incorrect view of marriage.

How could Renee change her thoughts so easily? She didn't know the truth. At the first signs of trouble, she panicked and allowed herself to repeat an old familiar pattern. Instead of seeking a biblical solution through godly counsel, she turned to well-meaning but equally ungrounded friends. She allowed herself to be deceived. The more she talked with those who viewed marriage contractually and who divorced as a solution to their unhappiness, the more she moved away from God's idea of covenant. The more she listened to the advice of disgruntled friends, the more convinced she was of leaving.

Renee isn't a bad person, and she never wanted to end up like her parents. She had the best intentions and even prepared for marriage in all the right ways but one—she didn't guard her mind. When her thinking grew confused, she didn't check her it against God's Word. Her fears drove her to people who didn't share her faith. So what she heard was contrary to the Word of God.

Many of you are like Renee—not quite sure what you believe. When difficulty comes, you are soft, pliable and seek out people who only tell you what you want to hear. Renee's friend wasn't trying to destroy her marriage. She thought she was giving good advice. At times it's helpful to hear how someone else handled a relationship problem. We don't feel so bad when we know other people have gone through a problem similar to ours. But you really must consider your advisor's belief system. The only important question is, "Does the advice line up with God's Word?" If it doesn't, ignore it.

What if Renee had spoken with a friend who believed in biblical covenant? Had the couple sought counsel from a Christian therapist, they would have been encouraged to be true to their faith and deal with Renee's fears.

Reject the Lie—Stand on the Truth

Marriage is a covenant between God and two people. Don't let any other view take root in your heart. Guard your heart. How? By knowing what God says about marital covenant. By rejecting the notion of marital contract. By seeking godly counsel. Will yourself to think what God thinks. Stand firm on the Truth. You may need therapy, but see someone who agrees with the covenant view of marriage. Marriage is a holy covenant—not a mere contract between two people.

Review

Lie #1

Marriage is a contract.

Truth #1

Marriage is a covenant designed by God.

Divorce-Proofing Strategies

- Change your thinking. Marriage is a *covenant*—not a breakable *contract*.

- Get help if your marriage is in trouble. See a therapist who will support the biblical view of marital covenant, preferably someone who has a track record of honoring his or her own marital covenant.

- Extend unconditional love to your partner as modeled by Christ. This requires patience, forgiveness, compassion and empowerment. This does not mean you overlook problems. It does mean your response to problems needs to be godly.

- Pray for restoration so you can honor your covenant.

- Believe it is possible.

CHAPTER 4

Family Matters

Lie #2

I married you, not your family!

This is really crazy—I married my husband without ever meeting his family. I met them the week of our wedding! Not a smart move. You don't marry someone without getting to know the family. Why? Because when you marry, the rest of the family comes in the deal—whether you want them or not. When I married, I had no understanding of this. I thought love was love, and families had little to do with couple bliss. I was naive.

Before you imagine some horrible reason why I never met my husband-to-be's family, I have a great excuse. At least it seemed like a great excuse at the time. His family lived halfway around the world in Argentina. I figured, *They're missionaries, how bad could they be? I mean really, they couldn't be preaching the gospel and ax-murdering people in their spare time.* At least that was my hope. Fortunately, it all worked out.

Still this was not a smart step. Meet the family *before* the wedding. It saves a lot of grief on the back end. Your spouse's family is more a part of your relationship than you probably care to believe. Spend time and get to know them prior to any commitment. Pay attention to family matters in order to divorce-proof your marriage. Here's why.

You're Sleeping With Five Other People!

Consider this lovely thought—there are at least six people in your marital bed! Now don't go checking for bodies. They aren't there physically. (If they are, we *really* need to talk.) Two families are emotionally present—you and your parents, and your spouse and his/her parents. And if your spouse has siblings, the bed is even more crowded—there is an entire family system joining you in marriage.

Most of you probably didn't pay that much attention to your spouse's family when you married. If you did, no doubt it was only for a second. If you were like me, you didn't concern yourself at all with how the extended family behaved. After all, you were enamored with your new love. You only had to put up with the larger group on special occasions.

While extended families may not be physically present in our homes, they do show up in the thoughts, beliefs and actions of our spouse. We act in ways that support what we've learned growing up. Sometimes though, we rebel and try to oppose that training. The process of becoming "you" involves integrating parts of the family into who you are. We take on good parts and not-so-good parts. It's the "not-so-good parts" that usually cause problems.

Family Matters

While we try to integrate all the parts of self into a whole person, we must also work on separating from our extended family. This emotional and physical separation is tricky business. It takes great skill to be your own unique person while still remaining attached to the larger extended family. The better you are able to separate emotionally and still keep your family connection, the better marital partner you will make. It is necessary to develop a strong sense of self. Otherwise you'll expect your partner to complete the missing parts.

Find the "I," Then Develop the "We"

Joe and Robin married young. They were both angry with their families for different reasons. Robin's dad was alcoholic. Joe's mom, chronically ill. Every night when Robin's father drank, the family's terror began. Some nights he would fall asleep and bother no one. Other nights he lashed out at his wife with verbal assaults and threats to hurt her. Robin quickly hid in her room, trying to avoid her dad's drunken rage. Fortunately he didn't seem to notice she was never around. Valerie, her older sister, was not so fortunate. Valerie became the new target of his alcoholic assaults; verbal humiliations were followed by physical brutality.

When Joe asked Robin to marry him, her yes was immediate. She desperately wanted to escape her unpredictable and abusive house.

Joe's mother was ill most of his childhood. She had a progressive disease that eventually left her bedridden. His father worked long hours of overtime trying to pay the medical bills. He rarely spent time with his two sons, but counted on their contributions to the family income as soon as they could. As the older son, Joe felt responsible to help his dad.

He dropped out of school to take a full-time job. Eventually his mother died, and Joe found himself working even longer hours. His youth spent on the family crisis, Robin distracted him from the pain and made him feel complete.

Early on Joe and Robin began to drift apart. Soon they were contemplating divorce. The therapist easily identified the problem. Neither Joe nor Robin had developed a strong sense of who they were apart from their families. Nor did they know what they wanted. It was easier to blame each other rather than face their personal pains.

Joe never thought much about his own needs. He was too busy paying the family medical bills. He hoped Robin could read his mind to figure out his needs. Secretly, he hoped his wife would be the "nurturing mom" he never had.

Robin also had no idea what her needs or desires were. She spent most of her childhood staying out of the way of an unpredictable drunk. Joe didn't drink, but he was a workaholic. Something about the way he ignored her felt familiar. How could she realize that she hoped Joe would be the "attentive dad" she never had.

Joe and Robin did what many couples do—unconsciously marry hoping the new person will complete missing parts within themselves. When it doesn't happen, they divorce.

The work for Joe and Robin was significant. Both had to define who they were apart from their family system. They had to tackle family issues—not avoid them. Then they had to grieve what they felt they didn't get, forgive their parents and figure out how the family influenced their own development. Joe and Robin had to discover who they were before they could accurately assess their marriage. Divorce was not the answer. They needed to find their individual "I" and then develop a "We." When you have a "We" with no "I," trouble begins.

Truth #2

You don't marry only your spouse —you get a package deal.

As you grow up in a family you learn patterns of behavior that will stay with you always unless you work to change them. You spend your childhood and adolescent years defining who you will become. Your individuality emerges from family relationships. Family isn't the only influence, but it is a substantial one.

Developing individuality requires emotional work. You need to become a separate person while staying connected to your family. How you manage individuality and togetherness matters; you must find yourself, but not lose your attachment. This isn't an easy task for most people. But finding a balance between individuality and family connection is a key to preventing divorce.

This balance is difficult to achieve because of family emotional ties. Families can be powerful systems of intense emotion and loyalty. Do any of the following statements sound familiar? These keep people stuck in the separation process.

- You feel guilty if you pull away, have your own thoughts or do things differently.

- You feel obligated to take care of weaker family members.

- You decide to guard dangerous family secrets out of loyalty to the group.

- You are afraid to leave home.

- You are angry about certain family matters and consequently want nothing to do with family members.

The balance between separation and connection is difficult to achieve because family members have interpersonal power. Strong personalities can overwhelm. Alliances can form. Siblings can gang up on one another. Subgroups form. Members can abuse power and play on emotions in unhealthy ways. You want to be emotionally close and yet not so close you lose sight of who you are. On the other hand, you cannot achieve separation by avoiding your family.

Separate but Attached

Your ability to extricate yourself from your family system and to function as a separate person has to do with how well your parents did this. If your parents balanced the closeness/separate scale, you will learn to do the same. If, on the other hand, your parents were unable to define themselves, were highly reactive to one another or emotionally detached, you will be in a similar position. Basically, your separate identity is determined by how well your parents defined themselves in their families while growing up.

If this is depressing, here's another sobering thought. *Most people marry someone who has the same level of self-definition as they do.* It may not look that way on the surface. Here's the classic belief: "I'm very dependent on my family, but I married an independent guy."

In reality, this is what usually happens: One of you copes with family problems by pulling away, the other by getting stuck in the togetherness. You find each other because both of you lack a good, clear sense of self. One is not more defined than the other. You simply cope with opposite styles. The dependent person envies the distant one, and vice versa. The two attract each other because they want what the other has (connection or distance).

Maturing through your teen and young adult years involves taking steps toward becoming a separate person from your family. As you grow into young adulthood, eventually you leave the family system and make your own way in the world (at least that is the hope). This process of leaving home is not only a physical step, but an emotional and spiritual one as well. The more you have developed a whole sense of who you are, the better marriage partner you will make.

You are healthier, and you will be attracted to someone who is also separate but attached at the same level. You will also have a good idea of how to maintain your self-identity while being in a relationship. This is a good thing. Problems emerge when that separation process gets stuck. There are two ways that could happen—either you cut off family relationships, thinking that is a good way to become independent, or you become overly dependent and have no sense of self-identity. The "I" is missing, and you go looking for a "we." Let's take a look at both responses.

Emotional cut-off

Some people confuse independence with emotional cut-off. They don't talk much with their families. They have little contact and deal with family relationships by *not* dealing with them. These people may look independent but aren't. They have not learned family connection. As a result, family members are emotionally or physically cut off. When conflict arises, family members do not deal with it. They distance. When things get tense, they check out. The emotionally cut-off guy may look strong and independent to a dependent woman, but he's not. He copes by getting away from people. Can you guess? These people have relationship problems.

People who cut off have little involvement with their original families. They usually do their own thing and don't turn to family members for support. They don't use each other to problem-solve. Cut-off is an extreme reaction to the problem of balancing the emotional and intellectual self.

Sticky togetherness

The other extreme is being raised in a family in which you never develop a sense of self because everyone has the same "groupthink." The family message is that you aren't supposed to have independent thoughts. Consequently you never develop your own voice. You are completely reactive to people in your family and can't maintain a sense of self or a separate "I." When emotions run high and conflict comes, you stay loyal to the family at all costs. Since you don't know what you think or feel, you tend to be easily influenced by others.

In these families, members have strong emotional bonds with each other. Loyalty to the family is demanded. Excessive closeness is the glue that sticks everyone together. People are overly dependent on one another and typically overreact to one another. There is little personal separateness. Basically, you have too much of a good thing. You are so connected you don't know where you stop and the other person begins. You have trouble setting boundaries, making decisions, developing your own interests and being alone. You can guess . . . these people also have trouble in relationships.

When Cut-Off Harry Meets Sticky Sally

You need help when you operate in one of the two extremes—too much stickiness or too much detachment. What often happens is the cut-off person finds the sticky person. The cut-off person is attracted to the closeness (even though it's too much) of the sticky person, and the sticky person is attracted to the independence (even though it's too detached) of the cut-off person. They see something in the other they wish they had. But as you learned above, both struggle with separation and attachment. Neither is better than the other.

Consider the story of Harry and Sally. (No, not the movie couple—I just like the names.) It's typical of many couples who have relationship problems. Harry grew up in a family with two boys, a mother and father. As the younger of two, he always felt somewhat lost and neglected. Harry's father was a rigid man who saw most things in black or white.

When Harry's dad reached the age of eighteen, he wanted out of his lonely house. His father (Harry's grandfather) was an alcoholic and drank most nights. His grandmother was depressed and stayed in her room to avoid her husband. Harry's dad joined the Marines and did well. His ability to deny his feelings and put them on a shelf was reinforced in the military. There he could be emotionless and thrive. Emotions served no purpose. He had to take care of himself and not whine about it.

Harry's mom, Alice, was a pleasant but sad woman. She rarely talked about her needs and did whatever her husband asked.

Alice grew up in a home with an anxious mother who was dependent on others to take care of her. Alice's dad left when she was three years old. Her mother never recovered from his absence. She cried constantly, and Alice felt responsible for her mother's unhappiness. She quickly learned not to have needs, too busy trying to keep her mother from becoming suicidal.

Harry's family moved often because of his father's military position. His older brother, Billy, seemed to enjoy the moves. He was an extrovert who made friends easily. He was also athletic and a good student, so change was easier for Billy. Harry, on the other hand, was shy and not so athletic. He hated moving because it was hard to make friends and try to fit in with new activities. Harry spent a lot of time alone in his room.

Neither of Harry's parents knew how to help their son adjust emotionally to change. Harry's dad told him not to be a wimp. His mom just cried, saying she felt like she was falling apart, too.

When Harry graduated from high school he started working at a local gas station. His father pressured him to join the military, stating it would toughen him up—make a man out of him. His mother rarely said a word and spent most days alone in her bedroom. When Harry met Sally, he thought she could fill the missing hole in his heart.

Sally came from a large family. The family laughed, cried and spent time together, lots of time together. Harry enjoyed the excitement of Sally's family gatherings even if they were a little intense. People shouted, yelled, argued and sometimes became drunk, but they seemed to want to be together. Sally was very close to her mother and father. In fact, her father gave her constant advice on how to live her life. In fact, everyone in Sally's family had an opinion about how Sally should be. She just laughed about it. So did Harry.

Soon after Harry and Sally married, they discovered problems. Harry was upset that Sally called her mother every day. He didn't want her family knowing their business. Sally told her family about the couple's financial problems.

Sally was mad at Harry because his family never called. She felt cheated in the relationship. His family didn't know her and didn't seem to care. She couldn't fathom how months would pass without Harry calling his parents. She also began to feel a cool distance from Harry. So, Sally began to complain about her in-laws. Eventually her complaints included Harry as well. "You are just like your father—distant and cold. But I'm not like your mother. I'm going to speak up."

As the tension mounted, Harry spent more of his time at work. He avoided going home and being alone with his wife, knowing she would complain about his emotional aloofness. Why hear it? It only made him feel bad.

Harry and Sally saw a therapist. They were headed for divorce. In therapy, Harry began to realize his father had always been emotionally aloof. Because his dad had to work and help out the family when growing up, he had little time to be a child. The emotional cut-off was generational. Harry's father learned to cut off his feelings, and he passed that pattern on to his son. Dad didn't know how to teach his son to grow emotionally because no one had helped him. He expected Harry to "deal with it" on his own–anything less was "whining about what couldn't be changed." Now Harry was acting just like his dad. He was distancing himself from Sally.

Sally's tight-knit family created problems for her as well. Her own grandmother had babied her mom since she had almost died as a child. Grandmother was always afraid Sally's mother would die. Consequently she was overly attentive.

Not surprisingly, when Sally was a child, her mother feared she might become ill and die. Sally picked up on that fear. She learned to be loyal to her mom at all costs, keeping her informed and reassured that she was well. Sally's stickiness was born in fear, fear that something out of her control could happen. She needed the support of her family; that's what saved her mother. For Sally, family ties were vital. The problem was that Sally's closeness was sticky–too sticky.

When Harry met Sally, he brought his generational pattern of emotional cut-off to the marriage, while Sally brought her strong need for togetherness. Each was too extreme in their reactions; each lacked balance.

For Harry and Sally to divorce-proof their marriage, changes were essential. Harry had to develop emotional closeness, and Sally, more autonomy. If they could strike a good balance they could use their skills to help one another.

Making Changes

How do you balance togetherness and separateness? Start by deciding where you fall on a continuum from cut-off to sticky.

Cut-off–––––––––––Balance–––––––––––Stickiness

Divorce Proofing Your Marriage

The closer to the midpoint you are on that imaginary line, the better. If you aren't sure where you are, consider this:

If you answer the following questions "yes," you are on the sticky side:

1 Do I involve my family in intimate issues?

2 Do I ask my parents for constant advice?

3 Do I wonder who I am away from my family system?

4 Do I need my family's support in order to survive?

5 Am I more loyal to my family than my spouse?

6 Do I have trouble with boundaries?

7 Do I have few independent thoughts?

8 Do I need to speak with my parents daily or constantly need people around me?

9 Do I need a lot of constant reassurance from my family that I did the right thing?

10 Do I feel more bonded to my family than to my spouse?

If you answer the following questions "yes," you are more on the cut-off end.

1 Do I have little contact with my original family?

2 Do I spend holidays, birthdays and important events with only with my spouse or my spouse's family?

3 Do I avoid resolving conflict?

4 Do I walk away from arguments or tense discussions?

5 Do I pride myself on not needing my family or showing them how successful I am without them?

6 Do I only hear from my family in times of crisis?

7 Do I wish I had different relatives?

8 Do I keep intimate thoughts and feelings to myself?

9 Do I expect to handle every situation by myself?

10 Do I hold on to painful issues that have never been acknowledged?

If you find yourself leaning toward one end or the other, here are ways to begin to effect change.

Suggestions for those who are cut off

○○ **Force yourself to be more involved with your original family.** Call them, talk to them and be concerned about what is happening to the people with whom you once lived. You don't have to move back home or become their best friend, but make efforts to be interactive. It won't be easy or feel comfortable. The more you force yourself to be involved with your original family, the easier it will be with your partner. Why? Because you will learn to talk, resolve conflicts, control your emotions and extend grace–all skills you failed to practice growing up that you need now.

○○ **Don't cut off when things get tense.** Your impulse will be to shut down or avoid problems when they arise. Don't do this. Don't give yourself an out. Determine to resolve issues no matter how much you want to avoid them.

○○ **Learn conflict resolution skills.** Specifically, learn how to problem-solve and negotiate with others. You may need to become more flexible and less rigid. When you don't like what's happening or don't get your way, learn to release the need to control. Focus more on partnering rather than opposing. Face fears of intimacy—Will I be rejected if I try to get close? Will I get hurt? Will I look foolish? Will I know what to do?

- **Share activities and interests.** Don't spend all your time doing things alone. Engage your spouse in your life. Invite your family to join you in an activity. Have them over for dinner, play a game, watch a movie—start with just one idea, and then let it grow.

- **Turn to your family for support and problem solving.** Learn to let others support you. You don't have to be the Lone Ranger. Even he had Tonto! In order to build family support, you must communicate how you are doing. This requires a degree of openness and vulnerability.

- **If you have cut off for reasons of abuse, don't accept the abusive behavior. You may be able to make a new appropriate connection.** I am not suggesting you allow abuse or ignore it. Sometimes when you confront abuse, family members will cut you off. But I am suggesting that with appropriate boundaries and zero tolerance for abuse, a new connection may be possible. It's always a good idea to work with a trained mental health professional when dealing with any type of abuse and family dynamics. There are so many issues to consider, and your safety is of utmost importance.

Family Matters

Suggestions for too much stickiness

⊙ **Find your voice.** Form an opinion and express it. Try this no matter how uncomfortable it feels. Don't just agree with someone unless you really do. Think about what you feel deep down inside. Know what you know. It may take work to identify your thoughts and feelings and then to express them. People around you may not always like who you are, but that's part of the process. Speak up.

⊙ **Do things apart from others.** Don't be afraid to be alone or do things apart from the family. You don't need people 24/7. If you do, then you need more work on pulling out of the emotional stickiness. You are more competent than you realize. Use your abilities and skills to shine.

⊙ **Set boundaries.** Your main allegiance is to your spouse–not to your original family or your friends. Don't tell them every time you breathe. Don't involve everyone in your business. Develop a strong couple unit.

⊙ **Don't look to others for approval.** Your family taught you what they could. Now you have to decide what is right and act on it. You don't need their approval–or anyone else's. Work on pleasing God. Do what He tells you to do, and you will be headed in the right direction. He is your ultimate authority; He has given many guidelines on how to conduct yourself in relationships.

⊙ **Think, and don't let your emotions overpower you.** When stress comes, don't let your emotions run you. Use your head to manage your emotions. It's human to have emotions, but making decisions based on them is dangerous because they're unreliable. Learn to balance your emotions and your intellect.

Is All This Work Really Necessary?

The answer is yes—all this work is necessary to have a strong marital relationship. If you don't define who you are before the marriage, you will have to do it during the marriage. If you do it before you get married, you will most likely find a healthier partner. If you wait until you are married, both of you will most likely have to work on this issue. Self-definition work can be accomplished within marriage—it's just a little more difficult because you are dealing with your "stuff" and your spouse's "stuff" at the same time.

The lie couples believe is that they must separate or divorce so they can find themselves. Discovering your "I" within marriage is possible with the help of a competent marriage counselor. Occasionally a therapist will recommend separation just to sort out the stickiness. But the intent is to work on self-definition fully expecting to reconcile.

Remember what I said at the beginning of this chapter— when you married your spouse, you married the entire family. Marriage is a package deal. Let's explore this notion a little more.

Marriage joins two *family systems,* not just *two people.* Imagine Jones is interested in Smith. The Jones family sends out a family representative, and that representative meets Smith, also a family representative. Jones and Smith date. They fall in love and marry. These two family representatives unite their two families. This can be a wonderful blending of two systems OR, as some of you know, not so wonderful.

You are a product of the environment in which you grew up. That family provided a prototype for future relationships. They taught you how to trust, how to deal with conflict, how to treat women, how to deal with failure and so on. You learned healthy ways to relate, dysfunctional ways or a combination of both. If you learned dysfunctional ways, you're probably experiencing relationship problems now.

Don't despair. Being raised with dysfunction doesn't doom you to divorce or disastrous relationships. Almost everybody was raised with some amount of dysfunction. There is no perfect family. If you came from one, you are not from this planet.

But become aware of what your family taught you. Then decide to keep the healthy parts and discard those parts that cause trouble.

Who Cares About My Family—I'm Married Now

You may be thinking, *Who cares about my extended family? I'm married now. They don't have any influence over me now that I live away from home.* If these are your thoughts, change them! Your extended family did—and does—exert tremendous influence upon the person you have become. Your ability to be intimate is determined, in part, by early family experiences. Problems arise when you deny this influence.

If you believe your family has no bearing on current problems or that you are nothing like your father or mother, you are living in denial. The similarities are often remarkable whether you admit to them or not.

My favorite coffee mug is one that has a very frightened and stunned woman screaming, "Eeeek! I am my mother." Buy this mug and look at it every morning! Once you recognize the similarities between you and your family, you'll begin to do something about them if you need to. If you had a wonderful mother or father, pause and give thanks now.

Now here's some good news. Your original family does not *determine* your future relationships. You are not a *victim* of that system. Even if your family was nuts, you aren't doomed to be nuts—you just may need to work real hard at not being nuts! You can learn to be different.

Identify the Baggage—Mine Is the Big Bag Over in the Corner!

Divorce-proofing begins when you become aware that you bring family baggage to any relationship. Then you must work hard to avoid potential problems. How do you do this?

Upon arrival at a destination's airport, you go to the baggage claim and identify your bags. You pull them off the carousel and claim them as your own. Bulky or heavy, they're yours, and you lug them to the next stop.

When you leave your original family home, baggage goes with you to the next stop of marriage. It's checked whether you claim it or not. All I want you to do is claim it so you can begin to unload it.

The purpose of understanding your family baggage is not so you can blame it, kick it, get mad at it or wish it ill. To understand the baggage is to understand yourself better. Did you get a bag that you like? Which bags need to be discarded? You can work on the parts you don't like, then dump that baggage. When you do, you'll make a better relationship partner.

Generational Patterns

Family members learn by watching each other's specific ways—and they take that learned behavior with them into their own marriages. For example, when your father yelled at your mother, you watched this and learned that it is OK for a man to yell at a woman. A girl who watched her mother avoid arguments will probably do the same. These interactional patterns are passed down through the generations.

Generational patterns are learned and rehearsed by family members over years. It doesn't matter whether you like the patterns or even if you think they are unhealthy. Most people repeat and reinforce them anyway. This is why problem people hook up with other problem people. On some level, people with problems are more comfortable with other people with problems. It's what they know, what they are used to, and it feels familiar.

Problem people do not band together because they like to experience pain! For example, women don't consciously say, "I grew up with an alcoholic dad so I'll find a man who is alcoholic." But when they are with alcoholic men, there is something familiar about them. And if they have never developed appropriate reactions to alcoholic Dad, they may end up with another candidate to work on (an alcoholic husband) until they get it right.

Here's another example: If you had a controlling, critical dad, you'll unconsciously choose a controlling man. Or conversely, you may so fear you'll marry a controlling man like your father that you find one at the other extreme—passive and uninterested.

This unconscious choosing also works in the positive. If, for example, you had a very affirming mother, you'll look for a woman who affirms you. If your father was involved in your day-to-day activities, you will look for an involved man. Understanding how families pass down patterns helps explain your relationship choices.

Your ability to distinguish between the thinking and feeling parts of you is also important. When emotions and intellect can't be separated, you function more poorly. You need a balance between the rational and the emotional. It's unhealthy to allow your emotions to rule at all times, or conversely, to be cut off from your emotions. Failure to achieve balance between thinking and feeling is also a generational inheritance.

The importance of recognizing your family baggage is major. Couples who have marital problems or want to divorce typically have not dealt with this aspect of their lives. They go through life saying, "I am who I am, and I can't change." (See Lie #7.) This is ridiculous, an excuse. If we couldn't make changes, there would be no hope for any of us. You must want to make changes. Have the courage to embrace your past in order to enjoy a better present.

Remember that you have the power to make changes in your life. You are not a victim of your family, but recognize their powerful influence on you. Deal with your past where it negatively influences your present. Claim your bags so you can sort through the laundry and lighten your load.

Review

Lie #2   *I married you, not your family!*

Truth #2   *You don't marry only your spouse— you get a package deal.*

Divorce-Proofing Strategies

I will . . .

- Develop a strong sense of self-definition by separating from my family of origin in a healthy way.

- Bring a well-defined "I" to the "we" of the relationship, or develop an "I" while in the "we" of the relationship.

- Identify the family baggage I bring to the relationship.

- Identify generational patterns.

- Work on changing the negative patterns.

- Find a balance between stickiness and emotional cut off by employing the strategies listed.

I won't . . .

- Blame my family for my present problems.

- Use my family as an excuse not to change.

Divorce Proofing Your Marriage

⚭ Cut my family off unless my safety or mental health is at stake.

⚭ Stay sticky.

CHAPTER 5

Rescue Fantasies

Lie #3

I can change my spouse.

I know Calvin is a little immature. He has a temper problem, but I will change him. He's never had anyone who loves him the way I do. Once he's with me, he'll calm down. I want to help him, and I know I can. I'm not worried about his uncontrolled anger."

"Whitney is a really great person once you look past her sexual problems. Her father never paid attention to her. All she needs is a guy who will care about the real Whitney and not just her sexuality. Once we get married, she'll settle down and stop flirting with other guys."

These two people are convinced their love will change their future spouses. And they are not alone in that belief. People marry, overlooking obvious red flags in the relationship because they are convinced their love will correct a multitude of problems. Unfortunately, this assumption is usually wrong.

Do you think you can change your spouse? If you do, you are headed for trouble. You can't force another person to change. You can try, but be prepared for disappointment and failure.

If you are already divorced, you know how difficult it is to try and change someone. If you are headed for divorce, you are probably struggling with this very issue right now. *If he would be more patient, more willing to talk, to try to deal with conflict . . . If she would show more sexual interest, stop complaining and take more time for me . . . If only . . .* is the mantra of your life. Guess what? It could be a long wait for "if only" to materialize. But that doesn't stop most people from trying.

Call in the TV Repairman

For twenty years I have watched people attempt to reinvent their partners. I have seen valiant efforts, creative styles, amazing feats and unreal persistence. Deep down people believe they can do what no one else has been able to do—change that intimate other. They think if they try hard enough, don't give up and initiate the right plan, change will happen. Occasionally, people have success. Apparently this occasional success is enough to keep trying!

Change is hard work. When it doesn't happen, unhappiness sets in. Unhappiness leads to growing dissatisfaction. And dissatisfaction can set the stage for divorce.

The unhappy spouse desperately wishes his/her partner would change. Eventually, that desperation includes a trip to my office. My assignment is to do what the unhappy spouse has been unable to do—make their partner change.

It's not uncommon for a frustrated spouse to drop off his/her partner in the therapy room, instruct me to fix the person and then send him/her back repaired. When this happens I feel like a TV repairman! "Here's the broken set, ma'am. Now fix 'er up and let me know when she's ready." The thinking is, *If my spouse would change, our marriage would be great. I can't seem to change him/her, so let a therapist try.*

Don't get me wrong. Therapy can help to create an atmosphere that fosters change. We'll learn what those things are in this chapter. But ultimately change is up to the willingness of each person. And an unwilling heart is a root cause of divorce.

Russ Wants to Change His Wife

Consider Russ. His complaint is that he married a slob. Russ loves his wife, but he is really bothered by her nonexistent cleaning habits. "My wife just doesn't care about our home. Everything is so messy. It drives me nuts. I grew up with a mother who kept order in the house. All I'm asking for is a little order. It doesn't matter what I say. Nothing changes. I'm starting to resent my wife." Russ longs for his clean mother (at least when it comes to picking up the house). His wife, in his mind, is not doing her job.

Russ isn't a bad guy for wanting a clean house. He just hasn't converted his wife to his view. She's refusing to be like his mother. So what is Russ's problem? He thinks his problem is his wife. Had he married a neatnick like his mother, he would be so happy. Or so he thinks.

Russ didn't marry his clean mother (although Russ's wife is a lot like his mother in other ways—see chapter 4). He married his wife, Jill, whose apartment was a mess when they were dating. Somehow Russ was able to overlook this flaw while they dated. He was convinced his love would change her habits. BIG MISTAKE! We will discover in chapter 7 that Russ was under the influence of romantic love.

In an effort to change his wife, Russ complains and makes digs about how sloppy Jill is. Obviously, this strategy isn't working because there is no improvement. The house isn't any cleaner. But like most people, he continues to use his tactic (complain) even though it has no effect on his wife's behavior. We call this *beating your head against a brick wall*. Ouch! Russ's head is so sore, but he keeps on doing it! Makes you wonder about Russ.

Finally, bloodied and wounded, he eventually gives up. All his effort yielded was an enormous headache. He also begins to resent his wife and to distance himself. Every time he walks into his messy house, it starts all over again. Russ gets upset, complains to his wife and nothing changes. Over time, he pulls farther and farther away emotionally. Eventually he thinks about leaving his wife. He's angry.

Russ's resentment, left unchecked, turns into contempt. Contempt is deadly in relationships.

Let's back up and look at how Russ might have avoided letting things get to this point. He applied the wrong solution to the cleaning problem. Instead of trying to make his wife change, he needed to change his own behavior. The only real control he has is over his own behavior and responses.

Forget the TV Repairman— Call in the Therapist

One solution Russ could try is to stop complaining since his complaints seem ineffective. OK, let's say he stops complaining. He still lives in a messy house and still feels resentful. Resentment left unchecked is also deadly.

Another possibility is that *he* could do the housework. This option gives him added benefits, since research shows that men who do housework have fewer physical problems, make better marriage partners and are less lonely.[1] Actually, it isn't the housework (I wish it were!) that strengthens marriage as much as it is the support men give to wives by pitching in with the housework. But Russ is overloaded with work and has no energy to vacuum after a long day at the office.

Russ could hire cleaning people. But Russ doesn't want to pay someone else to clean his house! He believes Jill has the time, and it's her contribution to the family. (Stay with me on this, even if you feel Russ needs enlightenment!)

Or (here's the one I usually opt for) Russ could try telling his wife about his growing resentment. Big deal, you say. How will that make a difference? Only if change occurs. It may not motivate Jill at all. On the other hand, Jill might be motivated by Russ's direct and honest feelings. He hasn't tried this approach. So instead of continuing to do something that doesn't work (complain), Russ changes his response.

Russ has control over this—what he says and does. What Russ doesn't know yet is when he changes his behavior (by being honest about resentment), he changes the interaction with his wife. He is no longer stuck in the old pattern— complain, nothing changes. Now he has a new solution. Let's see if it works.

Russ and Jill talk about his feelings. He resists blaming, concentrating instead on using "I" statements. "I get all worked up inside. I can't function. I feel stressed. It may sound picky, but a messy house makes me crazy." To Russ's amazement, Jill listens. (It's remarkable what good communication does!)

"Really?" she replies. "I thought you were just comparing me to your mother. It bothers you enough to make you crazy?" Then Jill tells Russ that she really doesn't like the messy house either. She feels overwhelmed trying to get everything accomplished in a day. Growing up she remembers her mother saying, "I'll trade a messy house for time with my kids any day." Jill tells Russ that she has been operating under this same philosophy. She has great memories because Mom spent time with her children. She hoped Russ would praise her choice, not be resentful of it. She thought she was doing the right thing.

Russ is surprised to learn how his wife feels. He assumed she was just a slob. He had no idea of her dilemma or frustration. While he admired Jill's dedication to the kids, he still hated the mess. He was clueless about his wife's inner struggle. He was also surprised to find the mess bothered Jill as well.

Jill's solution wasn't really working for her either. She wants to spend time with her children, but she can't stand the mess. (I'm real tempted here to suggest the cleaning ladies show up, but Russ and Jill are on a budget.)

I urge them to problem-solve a few alternatives. Russ asks if there are things he can do to ease Jill's burden (deep down, Russ is a nice guy). Jill is elated because she assumed (incorrectly) that she had to carry the cleaning burden since that's what her mom did. But it's a new millennium, and Russ reads the magazine headlines about sensitive men.

The couple begins to strategize on ways to spend time with children and get the house cleaned. Jill feels less threatened and begins to negotiate reasonable cleaning expectations. Russ has to lend a hand with the kids and pick up a few cleaning chores.

Now the couple better understands each other. They have corrected their misperceptions, and they negotiate new strategies that both feel good about. The solution came when they stopped blaming each other and started to think about what they could do to change the problem. Russ stopped wishing his wife would change and focused his efforts on his own behavior and feelings.

Russ and Jill are like most couples. They lock into specific marital patterns akin to a dance—Russ does this, then Jill does that. Their steps are usually the same. The dance becomes familiar and rehearsed. When problems emerge, new dance steps are rarely tried.

Here is Russ and Jill's marital dance: Russ's wife was messy. He complained. She ignored his complaints, feeling he didn't understand her. He didn't and became resentful. He pulled away, and she felt unsupported. Nothing got resolved, but they continued the dance.

When Russ made a new move (verbalized his growing resentment), the change process started. Russ and Jill began a dialogue. With the help of their therapist, they negotiated realistic expectations about housekeeping. Not surprisingly, Jill also had hidden resentment concerning Russ's lack of family involvement.

All problems don't resolve this easily, but the point is this— you can change something in your relationship by changing *YOUR* response, *NOT* your partner's. Too often, spouses try to change the other person or try to make me, the therapist, change them. Usually, this is a losing proposition. Instead, change your behavior, and the interaction can't stay the same.

Truth #3

You can change only your part in the dance.

To help couples understand this notion of change, I usually ask them to stand up and dance in my office. I know this sounds a little strange, but dancing can actually help you understand how couples interact and stay stuck. I borrowed this dance metaphor from the book *The Dance of Anger*[2] by Harriet Lerner. I have recommended this book to hundreds of couples over the years because of this helpful metaphor.

I tell a couple to assume the dance position and carefully follow the steps of the other so the dance proceeds smoothly. When they are dancing together, I explain that this is how most of their interactions go—they have learned a well-developed set of moves with each other. He does _____. She does _____. Then he does _____. She does _____. This is how they have learned to relate to one another. Some couples have dramatic steps, and others move quietly in familiar patterns. All couples have well-developed dance steps that they know and follow.

Then I ask one spouse to change a step in the dance suddenly—create a new step. This disrupts the dance. Usually the partner resists because he/she is pulled in a new direction. The resistance continues until one person gives in and the dance either changes to something new or it falls back to the original form.

This is exactly what happens in relationships. We lock into familiar dances. Even when we are tired of the dance, bored and unfulfilled, we keep going. Like those old marathon dancers, some couples just keep dancing the same old dance until they collapse from exhaustion (divorce).

But when a spouse changes his or her behavior (the step in the dance), there is usually resistance from the other. Eventually someone has to give in to the new way, or the couple reverts to the old familiar dance. The secret to change is to hold your ground until the new dance develops. Don't revert to the old way.

Years ago I saw a couple who was stuck in an unhappy marital dance. He dealt with stress by distancing. She dealt with conflict by overeating and trying to get him to talk to her. Their dance was typical of many couples. The more she came after him, the more he distanced. The more she ate, the more he complained how unattractive she was becoming. So she became resentful and ate more, and they both stopped talking.

Since he was unwilling to make any changes (see chapter 9), I suggested she make the change. She was to stop complaining about his emotional distancing since it was changing nothing. Instead, I had her talk about her loneliness in the marriage and how sad she felt. She also agreed to take better care of her body and not eat when she was angry with her husband. This was something she could do. With therapy, she stopped overeating.

At first nothing changed. Daily, for a month, I had her repeat how lonely she felt. In fact, she learned to verbalize her loneliness in the marriage. As she did, her overeating diminished, and she began to lose weight.

Her husband grew angrier, resenting the new dance step. He didn't want to hear how his wife, Deb, felt. It made him nervous, like he was supposed to do something about it. He also noticed her weight loss and began to worry that other men would find her attractive. He noticed more confidence in his wife.

Deb felt the tension and was tempted to stop saying the things we rehearsed. I encouraged her to keep responding in the new way. He was resisting change and wanted to go back to the old familiar dance. But if Deb held her position, the dance would have to change.

She stood her ground, but his anger led to a temporary marital separation. I advised her not to panic. He was trying to force the old way. She should remain firm, loving and not resort to the old pattern of giving in and swallowing her feelings.

After just one week, he called. Deb was terrified he wanted to pursue divorce, but to her amazement, the opposite happened. He wanted to come home. He realized he needed to work on talking about his feelings. He agreed to go to therapy to learn how. He admitted feeling alone in the marriage but had never told his wife. Her new confidence and weight loss made him think twice. Maybe he had problems, too.

Change would be uncomfortable, but he missed his wife.

She was simply talking about her feelings and how his behavior affected her. He admitted not knowing how to give her what she needed. He felt inadequate. Deb knew she must verbalize her needs rather than swallowing them with food. With help, the couple could work things out.

Deb's step in the marital dance changed first. All her prior attempts to change her husband went nowhere. So she could change her response to him. When she did, the relationship changed. When one person changes the dance, the dance changes.

None of us married the perfect spouse. He or she does not exist, or is in hiding on some tropical island. Yet we have no trouble getting angry when our spouse acts less than perfect. Our natural instinct is to point out our partner's flaws and tell him or her how to behave. That's easier to do than to examine our own role in the dilemma. Consequently we get stuck in negative interaction cycles. We can't seem to break out of the awful, but familiar, dance. When we try, we quickly give in to the old way because of the resistance to change we feel. It's hard to change an old familiar dance.

The Wish to Be Re-parented

Not only do we want our partners to change, but we also expect them to make up for all the bad things that happened to us before we married. We enter marriage thinking, *This person will make the difference. He/she will heal all the broken places in my life. I'll get from him/her what I didn't get from my family. I'll get the good dad or the nurturing mom I never had.*

These thoughts aren't always conscious. Most people don't verbalize such insight at the time of marriage. But these thoughts lurk somewhere in the recesses of our minds. How many of you have thought, *I wish my spouse could give me what I need.*

Rescue Fantasies

As we learned in chapter 4, we are the product of healthy and not-so-healthy family systems. Our job, if we want to be healthy people, is to figure out how to keep the good parts of the family system and lose the not-so-good parts. Our partners struggle with the same self-growth. We can't change another person into the person we want just because we desire this. Our spouse cannot be forced to be the good parent we never had growing up.

Granted, when you are attracted to someone, you see things you really like and admire. For example, maybe he talks about your strengths, something your dad never did. Or she is sensitive to your mood, and your mother wasn't. Obviously, you enjoy experiencing these missing pieces from the past.

Problems arise when you look to that other person to complete who you are—to fill in those missing pieces. The secure person doesn't have to look outside himself or herself for completion. This doesn't mean a secure person is self-sufficient and not in need of intimacy. We all need other people, but we shouldn't depend on them for our deepest needs.

Some people are always looking to others for affirmation or to give them a sense of self. Others stay aloof for fear of being hurt. Some are compulsively self-reliant as a defense against being disappointed. Still others engage in excess care giving or care seeking as a way to find love and acceptance.

When we try to force a spouse into the good parent role and are let down, we become angry, hurt and upset. We take offense, and thus enter the four relationship killers—criticism, defensiveness, contempt and stonewalling.[3] (See chapter 7.) We leave convinced we married a loser who could never meet our needs. In truth, we are so focused on what *we* didn't get that *we* miss seeing *our spouse's needs*.

We may act like children in need of a good parent. Unconsciously, we look to our spouse to become that parent. Because we've been hurt, wounded or rejected growing up, we assume true love will fix all those hurts. When we discover that our partner also has hurts and places of wounding, we worry and think we should find someone else—someone who is whole, fixed and together. Many affairs begin with this lie: There is someone out there who will meet my needs better than my spouse.

When you are needy or vulnerable, it is more difficult to accept a spouse who is also needy or vulnerable. Yet needy people attract needy people. When their struggles become obvious, the blame begins. A woman whose father never said, "I love you," may say to her husband, "You aren't doing what I need done. I need a man who will tell me he loves me every day." A husband whose mother undermined his confidence may say, "I need a woman who will build my confidence. All you do is question my decisions." Each now looks to their spouse to change their history or fill in the missing gaps. But you can't change history! You can only grieve the losses and move on.

You can work on being a loving partner to your spouse, understand his or her places of wounding and do all you can to heal the hurt. But you can't become a replacement parent.

What *Can* I Do?

So how do you prevent yourself from expecting your spouse to change in order to meet all your needs?

Depend on God.

Sounds like a nice cliché, but read on. Many people give lip service to depending on God, but few actually do it. What does it mean to depend on God?

Unfortunately, some people think it means you never act for yourself. You don't use your talents and brains. You passively sit back and wait for God to act. For example, I've heard people say, "No, I didn't apply for that job because I'm depending on God." Or, "I can't confront my mom; I'm just depending on God to take care of it." Look, He gave you a brain, talent and a plan (the Bible). Use it to act, but depend on Him to be true to His Word. Your dependence is on His Word and His character. But don't stop using all He gave you.

Before you depend on someone, you should get to know that person. This holds true for God. How well do you know Him? If your answer is, "Not very well," then that would explain why you hesitate to trust Him. Read what He says. Trust Him and see what happens. Is He faithful, trustworthy, true to His Word? If the answer is *yes*, then put your full dependence on Him.

Because of His transforming power, it doesn't matter how awful your earthly parents were—or are. It matters in terms of the healing you may need, but you have a heavenly Father standing by, always ready to help. Go to Him anytime, any-place, as often as you need. He is the correction for bad parenting. God can re-parent you. This gives hope to all of us and diminishes the need for our spouses to make up what we missed. God restores what was lost. He is Abba Father, Daddy God.

If you have unmet needs, don't underestimate the power of prayer. God is able to do things we can't even imagine. We limit His intervention in our lives by not asking for His involvement. We have the potential for a relationship with a perfect being who is love—perfect love. You will search your entire life for this and never find it until you find God.

Too many of us don't depend on God because we confuse the attributes of our earthly parents with His. We transfer the hurts and wounds of our parents onto God. Or we have bad theology, which attributes bad things to God—*God wants to punish me; I'm waiting for the big ball to drop from the sky; God is mad at me; God wants me to suffer.*

We have to learn to distinguish the characteristics and

nature of God from those of our earthly parents. If your parents have godly attributes, you are blessed. If your parents didn't give you what you needed to grow into a strong, confident person, you still have hope. Come to know God as your heavenly Father, and develop an intimate relationship with Him. Contrary to many people's impression, God has time for you. He's interested in you and wants to be in relationship with you. Go for it.

Be your own good parent.

No, it's not a contradiction. You can also learn to be your own good parent. For example, don't wait for someone else to tell you that you did a great job. Tell yourself. This isn't arrogance. You can build your confidence and self-esteem. The more you do this for yourself, the less you will need it from another person.

Listen, it's great when others build our self-confidence. We all try to do this with our children. We want our children to grow up feeling strong and healthy, but sometimes that doesn't happen. When it doesn't, all hope isn't lost.

Self-parenting is another way to correct a negative childhood experience or adult rejection (e.g., divorce). Therapists often teach clients to pay attention to their own strengths, abilities and appropriate behavior. When you act in a godly way, pat yourself on the back. In other words, reinforce your own appropriate behavior. The Bible provides standards for living and behaving. Line up your thoughts and actions to those standards, and then rejoice at your success.

For example, John has a temper problem. He yells. But now he is learning to pay attention to the times he doesn't yell and remains calm. When he controls his temper, he should congratulate himself, thus reinforcing his efforts to change.

No one in John's family reinforced temper control. John's dad had a major temper, and he certainly didn't model self-control. Now John is faced with the challenge to change. He has to do it himself, asking God for the help he needs. Most likely no one will be coaching his change efforts. In a sense, he must become his own good parent. "I exercised self-control. That was good. God is pleased, and I have been obedient. Good job!"

Changing behavior is incredibly difficult, especially when we have developed negative habits. Huge doses of encouragement are needed to effect and sustain change. If we depend only on others to reinforce our efforts, we may be let down. Perhaps a teacher, a coach, a counselor, a friend or a spouse will provide this nurturing for you. But if you don't have someone around who is supportive, determine to do it anyway. Then don't be afraid to reward yourself in the process.

Become part of the correction, not someone who reinjures.
Having first told you to depend on God, and then to learn to parent yourself, I now want you to know that you can influence change in your partner. Problems from the past can be reenacted in your couple relationship. Or they can be corrected. You heal the past by consciously paying attention to the way you treat each other and then making necessary changes. To do this, both spouses have to be willing to listen to each other, to be empathetic about past hurtful experiences and then behave in healing ways.

One way to begin this process is to admit that you want your partner to help you. Then talk through what that help would require. It works like this:

Tell your spouse about areas in your life where you were hurt. For example, you were criticized and shamed for having an opinion; you were rarely complimented and feel insecure about your looks; you were emasculated because you weren't sports-minded. Both of you can list areas of woundings that arise when your spouse says or does certain things.

Next, identify things your spouse can do to help this wounded area feel better—give me a compliment on my appearance; praise me for my nonathletic accomplishments; value my opinion by thanking me for contributing my ideas.

Once you've identified the corrective behavior, ask your spouse if he or she is willing to be part of the corrective experience. Most people, once aware of the hurt they bring to the relationship, will want to practice the corrective behavior. In essence, they agree to be part of the healing process.

It's important to remember that this is a conscious effort to which you both agree. It's no longer an unconscious wish you secretly harbor that is regularly dashed when your partner lets you down or can't read your mind.

Therapists are often called upon to help couples practice this form of healing. The beauty of this strategy is that your partner becomes aware of the areas of wounding and agrees to be part of the correction. Of course, there are some people who refuse and continue to play on the vulnerabilities of their partners. These people need individual therapy.

Over the years I have seen great power released when couples help each other this way. You truly become an example of Christ to your spouse. Unconditional love, acceptance and positive regard are powerful tools that shape self-esteem and change relationships.

Jesus had such an impact on people when He walked the earth because of this great compassion. He healed all He touched. He spoke words of encouragement and taught us how to love one another.

Marriage is your opportunity to show the love of Christ to an intimate other. Yet we so often hide this love and are afraid to express what is deep inside of us by the Spirit. Be part of the healing—not wounding—of others. Start in your marriage.

Creating an Atmosphere for Change

Once you have recognized that you alone can change your behavior (and not the behavior of others), you become a change candidate through an intimate relationship with God. You'll begin to correct your own behavior. You'll engage your spouse in a conscious effort to correct past hurts, and you'll find ways to create an atmosphere of change in your relationship.

1. Set up positive exchanges.

Remember, change occurs more often in the presence of positive exchanges. When you praise a child for doing things you like and want to build, you are increasing the likelihood that the child will make those changes. Adults are no different. If you praise even small movement in the right direction, you'll get change. Praise is powerful. It prepares the atmosphere for change.

Praise is practically nonexistent in the couples I see in therapy. By the time they come to my office, they are so focused on the wrongs and hurts that positive exchanges are rare. If you want change, start praising the things you like. Don't tell me there aren't any. You just aren't seeing the small and mundane things your partner does to make life easier. Build on those. Then when you see new behavior, reinforce it big time.

2. Work on yourself.

Spend less time blaming and more time working on conforming your life to the image of Christ. This is essential to prevent divorce. You have to identify your flaws and correct them, or you have no credibility telling your partner what to do. Often partners say, "He wants me to change, but he is so messed up himself." Or, "She points out my faults, but won't talk about hers."

Again, this unwillingness to see yourself as a work-in-progress creates resentment and resistance to change. Take responsibility for yourself first, then watch your partner follow suit.

3. Resolve conflict.

A predictor of divorce is the inability to resolve conflicts. In this book you will read about compatible styles and how to be an effective conflict resolver (chapter 6). Then determine to act. If you are somewhat uncomfortable with conflict, that's OK. We know this usually relates to your family experience. Conflict resolution is a skill that gets better and easier with practice.

Don't let things build up. This is unhealthy physically, spiritually and relationally. Agree with your partner to have regular checkups when it comes to disagreements and conflict. Ask, "How are we doing? Anything been bothering you that we haven't talked about lately?" Do this every day, or at least once a week, until you raise issues with regularity.

Conflict is part of every relationship. Your ability to resolve it makes the difference and fosters change.

4. Become more empathetic.

Willingness to change is encouraged when we feel heard and understood. Spouses are famous for stubbornly resisting change when they feel misunderstood. Your effort to intellectually identify and vicariously experience your spouse's thoughts, feelings and attitudes is called *empathy*.

How much empathy do you show? When I train rookie counselors, I assess their ability to be empathetic because it sets the atmosphere for change and isn't always present. People are far less defensive and far more willing to consider options when they are understood. When you put yourself in someone else's shoes and try to understand what they are going through, they are more willing to share from the heart.

Practice listening, and then repeat what your partner has said. Ask if you got it right and if you accurately reported what the person was feeling or experiencing. This won't be easy (you are learning a new skill), but it is worth the time. Empathy empowers change.

5. Lessen your dependence on the other.

No one person can meet all your needs all the time. Only God can do that, and since we don't physically live with Him yet, we are still dependent on others.

It's healthy to have friends to talk with, share activities and support. It's great when you can depend on friends, but balance is the key. When friends replace couple intimacy needs, it's not healthy. When others are your only source of support, the same is true. Balance your intimacy needs between your partner and friends. In the same way that you don't expect one of your friends to meet all your friendship needs, don't expect your husband or wife to meet all the other needs. Sexual, spiritual, deepest intimate needs—save those for God and your spouse. Friends can support and add to your intimate covenant relationships, but they should not replace them.

6. Take care of yourself.

Self-care is vital. Again, consider balance. Attending to your own physical, spiritual and emotional health creates an atmosphere for change. When you value you, others will, too. When you take care of yourself, the burden of worry is lifted from the other.

I have found many couples secretly angry over this issue of self-care. They resent their lack of self-care and erroneously blame their spouse for the same. When you spend yourself beyond reasonable limits, guilt often results. Many women don't know how to say no or take time for themselves. Many men don't nurture themselves spiritually or physically because they're too busy trying to succeed in life.

There is a difference between self-indulgence and self-care. Self-care is simply saying, "I need to be responsible for replenishing myself. I will see that it happens." When we do this, we are more centered and are better equipped to deal with change in our lives.

Review

Lie #3
I can change my spouse.

Truth #3
You can change only your part in the dance.

Divorce-Proofing Strategies

- Stop trying to change your partner. Refocus your efforts on changing your part of the dance.

- Examine the unconscious expectations you have for your spouse. Do you expect him or her to make up for all the hurts in your past?

- Become intimate with God and know Him as Abba Father.

- Reinforce your own change efforts.

- Be part of the healing—not hurting—process regarding past wounds.

- Create an atmosphere for change.

  1 Praise often.

  2 Resolve conflict.

  3 Become more empathetic.

Rescue Fantasies

⊙ Do not depend solely on your spouse for all your needs.

⊙ Take care of yourself physically, emotionally and spiritually.

CHAPTER 6

Dealing With Conflict

Lie #4

We are too different.

Since no two families are the same, no two people will get along perfectly. Coming to marriage from your unique family system insures you will have differences with your spouse. Unless you clone yourself, you will be in a relationship with someone who thinks, feels and acts differently. Granted, some relationships have more differences than others.

In my early days as a marriage and family therapist, I believed couple compatibility was the key to preventing divorce. If two people could agree on the important issues of life like religion, parenting and sex, and could talk sensibly about everything else, their marriage would be highly satisfying. Divorce just wouldn't happen.

So I worked very hard trying to help couples communicate

well and calmly address conflict. I was sure if they could just learn to be more empathetic toward each other and negotiate differences, they'd walk out of my office happy and ready to start their own couples' groups.

However, the longer I worked with all kinds of couples, the more I followed marital research and the longer I was married, my views began to change. Good communication and conflict resolution were not guarantees for marital bliss—as I once believed. Teaching couples how to talk nice and compromise was great seminar material, but it did not save many marriages.

Couple Disagreement Is Normal

Paige and Ben can calmly talk about their differences. "We don't agree on most things. All we do is fight. If I say black, she says white. It's like we thrive on conflict. And it seems most of our arguments never get resolved. I can't go on like this. I'm tired of fighting. I want out of this marriage."

"He always thinks he's right and has to have his way. He reminds me of my toddler son. I'm not going to agree with him when I think he's wrong."

"She has the craziest way of approaching things. I don't understand the way her brain works, so I make the decisions. I'm afraid we'll end up in a real jam if I don't take charge."

"How arrogant is that?! I don't agree with the way we spend money. I never used credit before I got married and don't like using it now. He buys everything on credit. We have been fighting over this ever since we said, 'I do.' If he doesn't start listening to me, I'll take my money and move out. It's that bad."

Welcome to the dialogue of couple disagreement. Sound familiar? If so, don't worry. You have lots of company. Couples disagree over all kinds of things from how to handle crazy Aunt Mary to deciding who goes first playing Yahtzee.

Dealing With Conflict

Usually couple disagreements fall into one of five major areas—money, sex, in-laws, parenting and household chores. There are many other things couples fight about, but these are the "biggies." If you get these resolved, the rest is a piece of cake! Right?

Since we all come from such a range of experiences and backgrounds, it's little wonder two married people have conflict. We've learned that family and life experience influence who we are, but so do gender, race and class. (See chapter 8.) We are unique. Wonderfully made! Our partner may or may not have an appreciation for that wonderfulness.

"It's ESPN or Me"

Paige flopped down on the therapy couch. "I've given Ben the ultimatum—it's ESPN or me. I'm worried he might choose ESPN. All he does is watch sports when he gets home from work. He doesn't talk to me or help with the kids. He sits in front of the television most nights flipping the remote from one cable channel to the next. It doesn't matter what team it is, just so it is a sporting event. I'm tired of this. I want a husband who cares more for me than ESPN."

"She's being ridiculous. She knew I liked sports when we got married. Watching a game helps me relax and takes my mind off work. When I yell at the teams, I blow off stress. That's all it is. We don't seem to do much at night anyway. The kids go to bed early, and she's usually busy doing something else. I don't see why watching TV is such a big deal."

"We've gone over this so many times, I don't want to talk about it anymore. Either he turns off the TV, or I'm leaving. It's that simple. I won't take a backseat to athletics."

"She's not being reasonable. I guess that's why we are here."

Paige and Ben disagree over television viewing, but they have a bigger problem. She wants his attention and companionship in the evenings. Ben wants to relax. Each has different needs. What they don't realize is that both needs could be met. The ESPN problem was solvable.

Once Ben understood that Paige's complaints were more about wanting to be with him, and she understood that he wanted to find a way to wind down after his job, we were on our way to solving this disagreement.

Here's what they agreed to do: Ben was to greet his wife when he came home and spend five to ten minutes talking about his day and asking about hers. Both parents did things with the children until their 8:30 P.M. bedtime. Then Ben and Paige did an activity together—played a game, looked at a photo album and so on. At 9:30 P.M. the TV was his. Paige didn't mind because she was tired and needed to get things ready for the next day. She valued her hour alone before bed to do whatever. The difference was she no longer resented Ben. Now he was spending time with her.

Not all problems are so easily solved. When differences are not understood or appreciated, they can lead to emotional distance. And emotional distance is a precursor to divorce.

Couples get stuck on specific problems—who will manage the money? How often should we have sex? Who will bathe the kids? Should Johnny's curfew be 11:00 P.M.? How should we handle cousin Jim the alcoholic? Generally the problems couples choose to fight about are irrelevant to divorce. It's the *way* they fight that is of concern. Couples' fighting styles typically *help* or *hinder* their feelings of love for one another.

The Calm Conflict Resolvers—Bill and Diane

I looked forward to my sessions with Bill and Diane. They actually wanted help. They wanted to learn how to deal with their differences. That's what brought them to therapy. After reading several self-help books and attending local seminars on marital communication, Bill and Diane were ready to hash out areas of disagreement. They were a therapist's dream couple–rational, calm, compliant and highly motivated to problem-solve. Rarely do I see couples this easy to work with.

Slowly and steadily, Bill and Diane worked on clearly defining their differences. They made lists. They worked on presenting their opinions in ways that were respectful and kind. "I" statements began to permeate their dialogue. (For example, "I don't like yelling at the kids. I feel bad afterward and out of control at the time. I want to do something else.") Carefully they refrained from slinging blame at the other. They were the textbook couple!

They learned to listen empathetically to each other, to understand each other, to help each other. Working as a team was empowering for both. Differences were worked out through by compromise. "No strife for life" was their silent mantra. What I noticed most about Bill and Diane was that they had compatible styles of relating. Both were calm and rational.

They worked hard when it came to smoothing out the rough places. Differences were evident but worked through to resolution. All it took was a little help in the right direction, and off they rode into the sunset of marital satisfaction.

For Bill and Diane, marital therapy worked just as my training predicted. All my years of marriage and family therapy study were paying off. We were all happy campers. I was certain Bill and Diane would live a long life committed to one another because they calmly worked out their differences. No big debate here–if you are like Bill and Diane, consider yourselves blessed and the coveted couple of every marriage therapist! But if you aren't, there's still hope.

Meet the Fighters–John and Mary

When John and Mary came to therapy, I pulled out my boxing gloves and took a deep breath. Time to referee. I knew the hour would be filled with shouting and interrupting. I had to be on top of my game and take charge. I wasn't interested in them spending my hour doing what they do so well without me—fight. In my office, they would learn to calm down and be respectful. I'd shape them up like Bill and Diane!

I observed how they related to one another. They argued about everything. It was high drama in my office. One outdid the other. Conversation usually turned into a shouting match.

"Oh yeah, remember the time you insulted my mother?"

"I never insulted your mother. She probably insulted me!"

"Yeah, well I remember it differently. You were making fun of my crazy family." (Both start laughing.)

"Stop it. My family's not crazy, just a little weird at times."

"Oh come on, you really don't believe that, do you?"

"You married me. Does that make me crazy, too?"

"I'm not saying you are crazy. I'm talking about dealing with your mother, who always has an opinion about how we raise our son."

"She's a mother, and I don't think she did so horribly with me. Do you?"

"Sometimes I wonder."

"Hey, that wasn't nice."

"Well, the truth hurts sometimes."

"Oh please, give me a break. What is your basic problem when it comes to my family? It's not like yours is a dream come true."

The shouting continues. Nothing gets resolved, and the volume rises. This lovely family discussion has apparently been repeated numerous times with no resolution. Mary likes her family and wants her mom's advice about child-rearing. John wants mom-in-law to bug out. The couple can't agree on the role of family in their relationship.

John and Mary revisit this issue weekly. Their conversation rarely produces an outcome, but they are highly entertaining.

Dealing With Conflict

This couple has fighting down to a fine art. And, I must say, each is equally talented.

Time to teach this couple how to communicate better and resolve their differences. "John, can you calmly tell Mary what you don't like about her discipline methods with your son? Wasn't that the problem that brought you to therapy?"

"Mary, listen to John carefully and repeat what he says so I know you heard it correctly."

"No, John, you say it using 'I' statements. Tell Mary what you want. Don't insult her family."

"Now, Mary, it's your turn to say what you would like. Please don't yell. I know you are upset. Just tell John . . . no, no, let's not argue again. Just tell him what you think is best, and John will tell us what he heard. Remember to use an 'I' statement."

All the while I'm thinking, *Is this really going to change anything? These two are not going to adopt this way of talking (I'm not even sure I would!). They will continue to fight no matter what I tell them. One argument somehow leads to another. But if they fight like this, they can't be happy, can they? Surely they'll end up divorced within the year.*

They only resolve things after they have dragged each other through the mud, and half the time there is no resolution. Isn't it my job to get them to talk to each other like two psychotherapists in training? The more they sound like me, the better they'll be. (Keep in mind, I'm young and naive at this point in my therapy career.)

No matter what I do, these two insist on arguing. Finally in frustration, I yell back and tell them to knock it off. "Knock what off?" John asks. "We are finally getting something accomplished here. You are helping us a lot."

"I am?"

We all start laughing.

John and Mary deal with their differences by fighting. They talk openly (some would say combatively). They sound angry and don't seem to acknowledge the other person's point of view. They are, by therapy standards, lousy communicators. But to their credit, they seem to have a genuine fondness for each other. Periodically through the fighting, they laugh and don't seem to take offense. They are OK with fighting as long as they can keep issues on the table. Resolving those issues is inconsequential.

What I didn't understand was that, like Bill and Diane, their *styles* of dealing with conflict were compatible. Both were fighters. At the end of the session, they shook my hand, told me what a terrific therapist I was and left the room. I was dumbfounded. They felt much better!

Honestly I didn't think this couple would last another two years. I imagined one would fall over from exhaustion or become deaf before they ironed out all their differences. If only I could have calmed them down and given them good communication tools. I failed to help them stop fighting. Surely they won't join Bill and Diane in the land of marital bliss! I was wrong. They're still together.

The Conflict Avoiders—Tony and Gail

Gail is madder than a hornet, but she is not saying a word. How do I know this? I see it all over her. She's breathing heavily, tapping her foot, shooting menacing glares at Tony and is ready to punch someone out. But she's not talking. She's not even moving or looking at him. Instead she has this weird smile on her face.

Tony, on the other hand, sits quietly on the couch, baffled by why he is seeing a marital therapist. "I don't understand why we are here. We have the normal problems most couples do, but we are OK. We love each other. I have no complaints."

"Then it's a mystery to me," I reply. Silence. Long silence. "So there is nothing I can help you both with? Nothing at all?" Silence again. Hey, I'm a patient therapist. I've an hour.

Still no discussion, although Gail is worrying me. She looks as if she'll explode any minute.

At our first session I learned that Gail doesn't explode with Tony. Instead she overeats. She is obese. Tony describes himself as a conscientious worker. From my observation, I'd put him in the workaholic category. Gail eats away her problems, and Tony avoids them by working. At first I failed to recognize that neither identifies these behaviors as problems. They only came to see me because their friend told them they needed to see a therapist. The friend was concerned that they rarely talked about their differences.

Tony and Gail don't talk about differences. They told me so. Both have learned to minimize conflict and, in fact, avoid it whenever possible. Tony said it best, "We've agreed to disagree. It's not a big deal that we don't talk about things. Gail and I get along OK. We've been married thirteen years. It can't be all that bad."

As a marital therapist I listened, but was thinking, *This is a dysfunctional couple who operates in denial. Tony and Gail are the opposite of our fighters, John and Mary. They must need my help. It can't be good for them to avoid conflict like this. Time to rescue this failing marriage even if they don't know they need rescuing.*

These two must learn to deal with their differences openly. Then Gail will stop overeating, and Tony will work less—even though neither has said they want help with these two areas of their life. Both of them acknowledge that they have never learned how to fight or disagree. It wasn't a safe thing to do growing up.

I figured it was my job to teach them how to talk calmly and rationally about their problems. You know . . . teach them how to be like me or like our dream couple, Bill and Diane. I have to save this marriage from disaster, right? Well, not exactly. Gail and Tony aren't going to divorce whether I teach them to communicate or not. I'm the one not tuned in to what's going on. I missed the obvious like with our previous couple. Tony and Gail also have compatible styles of dealing with conflict. They avoid.

Truth #4

Incompatibility or differences do not kill a relationship. How you work out those differences is what counts.

Why are these couples not headed for divorce? After all, we all know that communication and compatibility are keys to successful relationships. One couple fights, and the other avoids conflict. Surely these are formulas for divorce.

The answer lies in the findings of marital researcher John Gottman. Gottman and his colleagues at the University of Washington have been studying marital couples for years. He has published the results in several books and journals. What his research found was that *just because you fight or avoid conflict you aren't necessarily headed for divorce.*[1]

That you have differences with your spouse isn't such a big deal. Incompatibility or differences don't kill a relationship. The real issue is *how* you work out those differences. If you and your partner handle differences the same way or in the same style, you'll probably stay married.

The couples described above (the fighters, the avoiders and the calm conflict resolvers) will most likely stay married because they have compatible styles of dealing with their differences. Surprised? I was as a young therapist.

Early on in my career, I thought couples who fought all the time were headed for the divorce courts. I also thought couples who avoided conflict were doomed. So I thought I had to mold everyone into the calm, rational Bill and Diane couple. When I couldn't get them to behave calmly and rationally, I thought the marriage was destined to fail. I thought I failed. Fortunately, I was wrong.

The research shows that learning to agree nicely isn't what saves your marriage. Now don't get me wrong. I still think good communication is an admirable goal, as is resolving conflict. But neither will save your marriage.

To help divorce-proof your marriage you need compatible styles of dealing with differences. The styles of handling conflict must work for both people. OK, so the obvious next question is, "What happens to couples who don't deal with differences the same way (fighters with avoiders, avoiders with resolvers, resolvers with fighters)?"

The Mixed-Up Combinations— Bob and Carol, Ted and Alice

What happens when you have a conflict avoider like Bob who is married to a fighter like Carol? Carol says to me, "Maybe you can get him to talk. I sure can't. He's making me crazy. All he does is sit in his chair at night and read the paper. I want some attention. I deal with the kids all day. I'm tired. I want a break. He gets to go to work and come home and relax. When do I get to do that? I want him to pay attention to me, and all he does is read.

"I hate how I behave, but I'm desperate. I goad him. I call him names. I try anything, even if it's not nice, to get some reaction. But he doesn't react. Then I feel badly because of the things I've done and said, and he pulls away even more. Both of us feel rotten, yet we never get anything resolved."

Bob's response is, "Hey, she knew what I was like before she married me. This is who I am. I can't change that. (See Lie # 7.) I do the best I can." Bob refuses to fight. He wants to avoid conflict at all costs. When he thinks of fighting with his wife, he becomes physically sick. He watched his dad lose control, periodically slapping his mom and frequently lashing out at the kids. Bob won't become his dad. He won't fight. Better to keep quiet.

This couple is in trouble because they aren't compatible in how they settle their differences. One wants to fight. One wants to avoid. The end result is more emotional distance from Bob and more resentment from Carol. The more Bob avoids, the more critical Carol becomes.

Then there's Ted, who prides himself on being a calm rational guy. He wants to deal with things the minute they come up. "I can't live with strife. If something bothers me, I have to deal with it. Let's talk about it and come up with a solution so we can get the important things in life done. But Alice is so emotional, I can't reason with her. She won't talk. She just cries. I don't know what's wrong with her. Sometimes she just walks out of the room when I try to talk to her. How can we resolve anything that way? If she would just be reasonable."

Alice responds, "I can't talk to Ted. He scares me when he wants to talk about a problem. I know it's crazy, but if we talk about problems, won't things get worse? That's what happened in my family. After years of my dad's being unfaithful, my mom finally confronted him. She was calm but firm. After that, he walked out on the family. I used to think, *If she just hadn't said anything, my dad might have been around to be with me.* I missed him terribly. I don't want to disagree. I'm too afraid."

Ted and Alice have mixed-up styles of relating, too. Ted is a rational guy ready to resolve differences. But he married Alice, a conflict avoider. Theirs are incompatible styles of resolving conflict. Ted gets more upset as time goes by and begins to distance himself from Alice. Alice just cries and withdraws. Emotionally, these two are detaching from each other. This is not a good sign.

Dealing With Conflict

These mixed-up style couples usually have marital problems. If one of them doesn't make a change (which, by the way, is a lot of work, but possible), they will have trouble over the long haul.

They have to agree on *how they will resolve differences,* because the mixed-up styles lead to anger and frustration, which can turn nasty and eventually lead to emotional distance. Notice I keep reminding you that emotional detachment is a marriage killer.

One way to divorce-proof your marriage is to learn to resolve your differences using compatible styles. If you are an avoider, you may have to force yourself to bring up problems. If you are a fighter, you may have to calm down, take five, watch your mouth and speak in a reasonable tone. We know that people with similar styles stay married, especially if other things are present, too. What are those other things? You'll find out in chapter 7.

Take a moment, and think about your style of resolving differences. Don't get hung up on how much conflict you have or how well you communicate. Forget the lie that you and your spouse are too different. Remember, the important thing is how you deal with that conflict, not whether it exists or not!

Let me encourage you with this. I married an avoider. I am a fighter. The first time we hit a major conflict in our marriage, he walked away, and I went ballistic. We didn't get too far resolving anything. Intuitively (I was also in graduate school studying to be a therapist) we sat down and talked about how we would handle disagreements. He couldn't walk away, and I couldn't be histrionic! The compromise was that he would force himself to stay in the disagreement (contrary to his family background), and I would force myself to calm down and deal with the issue at hand (contrary to my family background). It worked. Twenty-six years later our styles have evolved together. Incompatible at the beginning, we now resolve differences with compatible styles.

Identify Your Style of Handling Differences

Identify your style. Are you a fighter, avoider or calm conflict resolver? Are you married to a fighter, avoider or calm resolver? Do you have compatible styles? If yes, skip ahead. If no, read on. One or both of you have to make changes in order to divorce-proof your marriage. Work on your style of dealing with differences using these suggestions:

- If you are an *avoider* married to a fighter or resolver, try to talk more about problems. Learn to assert yourself. Find your voice. Don't be afraid based on your past. (See chapter 4.) You may need counseling to help work through earlier experiences so that they don't replay in the present. Work on whatever is preventing you from attacking the issue.

- If you are a *fighter* married to an avoider or resolver, try to calm down. When you get in your fighting mode, take a ten-minute time-out to calm down and think. Count to ten slowly; breathe deeply so you can speak without yelling. Basically, learn calming techniques. Pray for self-control.

- If you are a *calm resolver* married to a fighter, don't get so upset if your spouse doesn't behave as you do. Recognize his or her need to be impassioned. You might try throwing a little emotion into the argument yourself.

- If you are a *calm resolver* married to an avoider, encourage him or her to tell you what's wrong. Reassure him or her that nothing bad will happen. You want to know what he or she thinks or feels. Make your relationship a safe place to bring up issues.

Decide how you will handle differences as a couple. Even

though you don't have to become calm and rational in your approach to *save* your marriage, I believe there is biblical reason to aim for this style.

Hey, That's Not What the Bible Says . . .

One of my favorite children's books is written by Bill Ross and titled *Hey, That's Not What The Bible Says*. The author tells a Bible story and then rewrites the ending so that it is not biblically correct. You (preferably your children) then turn the page to a bunch of kids yelling, "Hey, that's not what the Bible says," and the story is corrected.

Even though marital research tells us that fighters and avoiders with compatible styles will most likely stay together, we need to consider what the Bible has to say about dealing with differences. Like the kids in the book, we need to question the end to which this research takes us. Is it OK to be a fighter or an avoider as a Christian, or are we called to a higher standard? We may not divorce with these styles of dealing with differences, but are these styles compatible with biblical instruction concerning our individual character development?

What does the Bible say about conflict?

Biblically we are instructed to go to someone when we have a conflict (Matt. 18:15). We are told to resolve our differences. We should clear up hurt and anger so they don't take hold and become unforgiveness and bitterness (Eph. 4:26). Anger isn't wrong, but handled incorrectly it can be damaging.

Dealing with anger

Christians often believe that anger is wrong, and they use Scripture to try and justify their position. For example, I had a couple in therapy who had serious marital issues that were affecting their teenage daughter. The husband was an angry man whose clear unspoken message was that no one had permission to disagree with him. This message played into his daughter's development of bulimia. She couldn't openly take on her father, so she used food to secretly rebel.

The wife grew depressed, never openly challenging her husband even though she sensed that not dealing with him contributed to her daughter's distress. In therapy the wife made timid attempts to disagree. When she did, the husband would quote Scripture about her need to be a peacemaker. He used the Bible (incorrectly) to silence his wife.

His stance was based on a misconception that Christians are not supposed to be angry, a misconception that he, like so many Christians, learned as a child. So whenever there was a disagreement, he stopped it by quoting choice Scriptures. The daughter's bulimia was an attempt to rebel against this injunction and do what the mother could not do—find a vent for her anger.

Anger is not wrong. It is a God-given emotion. Emotions are simply mood responses to living your life. They are influenced by thoughts and behavior, and are unpredictable, positive *and* negative. They are a part of your human makeup. God didn't make a mistake and say, "Oops, I threw in anger when I created man. That was a mistake. Now what?"

Anger is an emotional response that occurs in relationships. For example, you may get angry when your husband forgets to take out the trash. Your wife may anger you when she is a backseat driver. To deny the feeling serves no purpose. In fact, it can lead to all kinds of physical and emotional difficulties, such as depression, eating disorders and alcohol and drug problems.

Jesus experienced a wide range of emotions while He lived on the earth—compassion, pity, grief, anguish and, yes, anger. He was angry when the Pharisees tried to trap Him in legalism and refused to recognize Him as the Messiah. He was angry with the moneychangers in the temple for making His Father's house a den of thieves.

Dealing With Conflict

Obviously, God knows that anger is a part of our emotional makeup, which is why He instructs us to "be angry, and do not sin" (Eph. 4:26). The first part of this scripture gives permission to be angry. Anger can be used to correct wrong and bring about change. But the mishandling of anger can be problematic. "Do not sin" means control this emotion and use it in productive—not destructive—ways.

Spiritually we are taught:

- *Be quick to hear, slow to speak, slow to anger; resolve anger before the sun goes down (James 1:19).* Whether you want to lash out or bury your anger deep inside, the instruction is to calm down and deal with the problem immediately. Things spoken hastily can hurt. Words are powerful and cannot be taken back. Think, listen and calm down before you react. Then deal with anger immediately, not weeks, months or even years later.

- *Don't give full vent to your anger (Prov. 29:11).* You may be angry, but you don't have license to unleash it on anyone or anything. Control your tongue and behavior. Self-control is a fruit of the Spirit. Cursing, hitting, breaking things and intimidating others are not godly behaviors.

- *Don't get caught up in name-calling (Matt. 5:22).* Name-calling and bullying are not Christlike behaviors. They are damaging and serve no purpose but to hurt the other person.

- *Don't take revenge on a violator (Rom. 12:19; Heb. 10:30).* We live in a culture of lawsuits and revenge. The Lord says vengeance is His and He will repay it. This isn't a popular position and very difficult to accept, but don't repay evil with evil. Marriages built on revenge are headed for divorce.

⚭ *Forgive those who anger you (Matt. 6:14).* Forgive others as Christ has forgiven you. It doesn't matter how justified you are in your position; if your spouse is wrong, you are to forgive. You didn't deserve Christ's forgiveness, but He gave it to you anyway. Now do the same for your spouse. Don't wait for him or her to ask for forgiveness.

⚭ *Get to the source of your anger (Ps. 139:23–24).* Search your heart and be honest. What are you really angry about? Whom are you judging? Ask the tough questions so that you can effectively deal with the root of your anger. You may have to think and pray about the actual source of anger, because sometimes it isn't immediately evident. Often in therapy couples will be angry with spouses, only to discover the true source dates back to past hurtful experiences. The spouse becomes the unwitting target of that hurt-turned-anger.

⚭ *Don't stay angry (Col. 3:8).* This is a key. Feel angry, try to resolve the problem and then move on. You can get physically and emotionally ill if you hang on to anger. Bitterness can develop and grow. Not everything in life is resolvable, so learn to let go.

⚭ *Give the anger to God (1 Pet. 5:7).* Ultimately, release anger to God; give it to Him. He tells us to cast all our cares on Him. He can handle it and do more to heal us than any apology or revenge could ever accomplish.

In addition to spiritual directives concerning anger, you need to take practical steps. Here are just a few to get you started. Many communities offer help for anger problems. Look for local seminars, workshops and classes on anger management. Talk to mentors, check out books and pray for the love of God to fill your heart so you can experience the fruit of the Spirit. Learn to control angry impulses.

- *Don't make excuses for your anger.* It's easy to say, "That's just the way I am" or "My father was like this and I learned it from him." Take responsibility. You are not a victim of people or circumstances. You are responsible for your own behavior no matter what.

- *Don't jump to conclusions.* Ask yourself, "Is my anger based on a real situation, or is my perception off?" Sometimes we misread our spouses even after we have been together a long time. We judge them incorrectly and hold on to upset. Clarify the situation and facts of an angry moment.

- *Don't let anger cover other emotions.* Anger can make you feel powerful and mask hurt and pain. Anger is a socially sanctioned emotion for men, while other emotions are viewed as less than masculine. Under the anger may lurk a disappointed or wounded soul.

- *Refuse to keep thinking about the injustice.* Many couples continue to ruminate on past problems, especially those in which they were treated unfairly. Let it go. Confront the issue, do what you can and then move on. Don't get stuck in anger.

- *Don't vent.* Research actually shows that when you express anger by screaming, yelling, punching pillows, raging or throwing tantrums, you actually increase anger rather than reduce it. Contrary to popular belief, ventilation does not make anger go away.

- *Choose to think on good things.* Force yourself to rehearse the good qualities and behaviors about your spouse.

If you dwell on negative qualities, your anger will increase.

Ⓢ *Do something physical like a sport to release anger from your physical body.* Take a walk, play racquetball or work out at the gym. These are appropriate ways to release physical tension.

Ⓢ *Be assertive and confrontational, but not aggressive.* More problems would be dealt with if people were kinder and less intimidating. Treat your spouse as you would treat a boss or respected person.

Ⓢ *Practice calming strategies.* Count to ten. Take a deep breath. Learn deep muscle relaxation and other physical and emotional strategies to calm and soothe you.

Ⓢ *Take a time-out.* It works for children and adults.

Ⓢ *Walk away temporarily.* This is a form of time-out and useful so long as you return to deal with the issue.

Ⓢ *Deal with underlying feelings of insecurity, low self-esteem and past hurts.* Many times the conflict between two spouses is a replay of past unresolved issues and individual insecurities. You may need counseling and a deep encounter with God, asking Him to reveal those areas of your life under reconstruction.

Resolving differences God's way

We are clearly told to resolve conflicts and settle disagreements. Spouses in the Bible had disagreements—Abraham and Sarah, as well as Jacob and Rachel, argued over childlessness. Job's wife disagreed when it came to dealing with his illness. Obviously, these weren't bad people. They simply had disagreements. Neither are you bad if you disagree with your spouse.

Dealing With Conflict

The biblical model is to face conflict, go to the person involved and talk about it, get a mediator if you need one and resolve it. This doesn't give you much of a case for conflict avoidance, does it? It also doesn't give you much of a case for uncontrolled fighting, because we are told to confront in gentleness and love.

If this isn't enough work, we have to forgive and move forward in our relationships. We are not to carry grudges. We are to live in peace. Not peace at any price, but peace brought about through gentle confrontation.

Forgiveness Is Part of the Process

Mary had a fight with her husband. In therapy she said she had forgiven him but was unwilling to reconcile the relationship. Is there a difference? What should the Christian response be toward her husband?

People get confused about the difference between forgiveness and reconciliation. They are not the same. The main difference is this: *Reconciliation* is something that happens between two people. *Forgiveness* is an individual process. Just because you forgive your partner doesn't mean you have reconciled with him or her. But Christ calls us to do both.

Forgiveness is a gift. You give to another person. Forgiveness not only releases the other person from an offense, but it also releases you from hanging on to that offense. It isn't always instantaneous. Hurtful words, actions and emotions have to heal over time. When you forgive, you must let go of negative emotion (anger, resentment) and negative thoughts (judgment) toward the person who hurt you. Forgiveness is an unconditional gift you extend, deserved or undeserved, because God gave it to you. That's the model of Christ.

Reconciliation is an interpersonal process that restores trust between two people. Mary was unwilling to work out differences with her husband. In order to reconcile, she would have to resolve or lay aside differences and mend the broken relationship.

Couples today are challenged to move beyond forgiveness toward reconciliation. When a break in the relationship occurs through conflict, divorce—not reconciliation—is too often pursued. Reconciliation requires a mutual restoring of trust between two people, which comes about through trust-worthy behaviors and interpersonal work. Forgiveness is just the first step in the process.

There are cases in which reconciliation is not desirable. When a spouse is abusive and dangerous and continues the behavior, the other spouse may forgive but decide not to reconcile based on safety issues. Ongoing abusers lack repentance. Physical danger is a reality.

For the Christian who is not in a dangerous relationship, it is not enough to resolve differences or forgive. Jesus calls us to be reconciled with one another (Matt 5:24), to restore our relationships with each other and live together in unity whenever possible. Determine in your heart to move beyond forgiveness. Honor your covenant, and work toward marital reconciliation.

Mary was right to forgive her husband for what he did. Now with God's help and her willingness, reconciliation is an achievable goal.

So remember, neither fighters nor avoiders are doomed to divorce. It's the way you handle differences that's important. God's way may be more difficult, but it's always the best way. Follow His principles and handle disagreements in love. If you need a good definition of love, look up 1 Corinthians 13. Was this passage read during your wedding ceremony?

And There Is More to This Story

Developing compatible styles of dealing with differences is only part of the story to divorce-proofing your marriage.

One other important point is not all couple problems are

fixable. Marriages can live and even thrive when couples learn to accept unsolvable differences. Look at marriages that have endured for years. Those couples are not perfect, and they most probably argue and disagree. Many have the same fights over and over but don't seem to grow apart because of their differences. They have learned to accept differences as a relationship fact.

We are all flawed, yet God loves each of us unconditionally. Unconditional love is the key. Certain personality traits are part of the "I do" package. Work on loving your partner as Christ loves you. If you come to a crossroads of difference that seems unsolvable, agree to disagree. Don't allow negative feelings to build, and don't continue to harp on the subject. Let's work harder to live with people who aren't exactly like us.

Review

Lie #4

We are too different.

Truth #4

Incompatibility or differences do not kill a relationship. How you work out those differences is what counts.

Divorce-Proofing Strategies

In order to divorce-proof my marriage I will:

- Identify my way and my spouse's way of handling differences.

- Develop a compatible style of handling differences using the suggestions in this chapter.

- Choose a biblical model that includes loving confrontation, control of my tongue and appropriate expression of anger.

- Get help and practice anger management if I have an anger problem.

- Choose to forgive differences, and reconcile the relationship.

- Agree to disagree over issues that seem unsolvable.

CHAPTER 7

Growing Apart

Lie #5

I've lost that loving feeling, and it's gone, gone, gone!

"I'm not in love with Julie anymore. In fact, I wonder if I ever really loved her at all." Jeff stared at his feet. "I don't want to be with her anymore. I feel nothing for her. This marriage is dead."

Quietly, Julie added, "I don't know how we got to this place. We barely speak. When we do, we have nothing good to say." Tears began to trickle down her cheeks. The pain was obvious. "So mostly we just ignore each other. Actually we've been living separate lives for a year or so. How did this happen? Is it possible to fall out of love with someone?"

When I pressed Julie and Jeff for examples of positive moments in their relationship, they drew blanks. All they could remember were nasty fights and unending complaints.

Jeff was the first to withdraw from the negativity. He began to distance himself, and eventually he just stopped caring.

As Jeff pulled away, Julie's panic manifested as increased criticism. She found herself screaming at him and calling him names. Nothing seemed to move him. The more he withdrew, the more she came at him with a flood of complaints. Emotionally, Jeff checked out. Julie became depressed.

Jeff and Julie are good candidates for divorce. They see no solution but to end their relationship and move on with life. They represent many couples who are emotionally disconnected. The feeling of love has eroded.

The question is, how did Jeff and Julie get to this point? Friends remember their dating, wedding and early years of marriage with fondness. Julie and Jeff certainly were in love once. Somehow they lost that loving feeling, and just as the song continues, "It's gone, gone, gone." If we look closer at their relationship and revisit Gottman's research, we'll find answers.

Gottman's studies tell us that the *quality* of the emotional relationship with your spouse is important. His findings are simple but vital to the health of any intimate relationship. When positive exchanges outweigh negative ones, relationships do well. More specifically, Gottman quantified this ratio of positive to negative interactions. It's a great guideline for couples.

Gottman's Five-to-One Rule

In the previous chapter I talked about the importance of compatible styles when dealing with differences. Gottman's research also tells us that couples must have a healthy ratio of positive moments to negative ones. After years of observing couples, Gottman and his colleagues found that for every negative moment, five positive ones are needed to balance the relationship. So, for example, if you and your spouse are both fighters, there must be many positive moments (five for every one) in your relationship when you are not fighting. If you are a passionate fighter, then be a passionate lover. If you tear down your spouse (which I prefer you don't do), build him or her up five times more.[1]

When Fighting Overtakes the Positives

Jeff and Julie were both fighters. At the beginning of their marriage, they got into heated arguments that often ended with passionate makeups. Jeff was highly attentive to Julie and big on romance. He sent her flowers and special notes, and he called often during the day just to hear her voice. She returned the positive attention with affection, humor and desire to meet Jeff's needs.

During the first five years of marriage, the number of positive exchanges greatly outweighed any negativity from fighting. But as stress started to mount, things changed. Jeff was passed up for an important promotion while Julie advanced in her job. A few months later, Julie's mom suffered a stroke and the recovery was slow.

Jeff and Julie still argued, but something changed related to the mounting stress. Instead of fighting over differences, their exchanges took on a personal negativity. They became sarcastic. Criticism became commonplace until both felt a rising dislike for the other. The friendship they both enjoyed at the beginning of their relationship quickly deteriorated into resentment and defensiveness.

Julie suspected Jeff envied her promotion. His jealousy took the form of put-downs and control. Jeff was grateful for the extra money Julie's promotion afforded, but he felt slighted when he was passed over at his company. He knew it was wrong, but he began to resent Julie's talent and looked for ways to make her look bad.

Julie was angry with Jeff for the insensitivity he showed

toward her mother's health problems. He complained that she spent too much time with her mom and ignored the needs of their family. He argued about her mom's dependence and insisted Julie demand that her other siblings become more involved. The stress of an ill mother and an angry husband wore on Julie. Overwhelmed, she tuned out Jeff's emotional needs. She resented his lack of support, and soon she began to resent him.

What resulted was a change that devastated the relationship. As a reaction to stress, Julie and Jeff started firing negative arrows at each other. Their aim became personal. All their frustrations were unleashed on each other. Eventually, the wounds were so deep they could no longer stand to be together. They had grown apart, their friendship dead.

When Conflict Avoidance Turns Deadly

Other couples may not fight like Jeff and Julie; instead, they avoid problems. As we learned in chapter 6, this doesn't mean death to the relationship. One reason couples stay married even when they avoid conflict is because positive moments outweigh the negative ones. Avoiders may be less passionate than fighters, but they are also less negative. Their homes are viewed as places of solace with enough good moments to override the bad.

"Good" for some people can be a quiet, calm atmosphere with the absence of negative things (hitting, drinking, name-calling). Even though some couples are afraid of disagreements and don't resolve issues, there are enough good things happening in the relationship to keep them satisfied.

But when conflict avoidance leads to feelings of anger, and a spouse holds secret criticism, this can become destructive. Take the case of Tom and Cindy.

Cindy grew up in an alcoholic home and learned at an

early age to keep her opinion to herself. If she disagreed with her father, he became violent and verbally lashed out.

Tom's parents pretended problems didn't exist. They refused to address most difficulties and suffered from a number of psychosomatic health problems. Tom learned to avoid conflict.

When Tom and Cindy's middle child began rebelling by partying and drinking, Cindy panicked. She feared her son would become an alcoholic like her father. Tom's response to his son's drinking was to do nothing. He told Cindy she was overreacting, that their son was just going through a teen phase and would be fine after the curiosity was over. Cindy was not convinced but said nothing.

As the couple's son became more problematic, Tom still refused to act. Cindy's anger mounted, and her thoughts toward her husband turned negative. She began to see him as a wimp–leaderless and irresponsible. She held these feelings inside, afraid to say anything. Tom continued to minimize their son's problems.

Over time, Cindy began to hate Tom for his inability to take charge. Her resentment grew, and she pulled away. One day, she announced that she was leaving. Tom was stunned. There had been no angry exchanges. What he didn't know was that Cindy's long-term resentment had grown into contempt. It was emotional disconnect time.

Their failure to tackle a serious problem with their son led Cindy down a destructive path. She chose to criticize her husband to the point of hating him for his inaction. However, she never confronted her negative feelings, and she watched the positives of the relationship slip to nothing.

Both Tom and Cindy were conflict avoiders, but under stress Cindy's feelings began to change. Her interactions with Tom grew more negative and her perception of him changed. Positive moments dwindled under the unresolved stress. Cindy's love for Tom began to fade.

As Cindy's feelings changed, positive interactions rarely

occurred. Most of Tom's behavior was filtered through a negative lens. Obviously the five-to-one rule was no longer operating.

If you feel you have lost love for your spouse, ask yourself these questions:

- ⊙⊙ Do we have more positive interactions in our relationship than negative ones?

- ⊙⊙ Do I generally like the person I married?

- ⊙⊙ Do I consider my partner a friend?

- ⊙⊙ Have I allowed negativity to build and take on a momentum of its own?

If negativity and negative interactions have gained momentum in your relationship, it's time to make changes. Once you begin to view your spouse as the enemy—and not your friend—you're in trouble. Once those negative exchanges outweigh positive ones, you start to check out emotionally. Over time, divorce becomes an option you willingly embrace.

Relationships, when placed under stress, can deteriorate because of failed expectations, lack of self-understanding, inappropriate blame, acting out and other destructive emotions and behaviors. When a partner allows the above to translate into ongoing negative exchanges, the relationship is in trouble.

Truth #5

That loving feeling can be restored.

To divorce-proof your marriage you must have more caring moments than uncaring ones. How do you accomplish this? By focusing on the positive aspects of your relationship. If you love to ride bikes, go ride them. If you enjoy good books, join a book club together. If you like to laugh, rent a funny movie. If you give great back rubs, give them often. If you like to hear you are loved, say it. Say what you like. Let your partner know, and then do it. Create caring moments. Or recall great memories from the time you dated. What first attracted you? How did you enjoy each other? Do more of that again!

You must keep the friendship part of your relationship strong. Spend time together, laugh and create happy memories. It is easy to allow busyness or boredom to take over your relationship. Make time to go for a walk, to go out on a date or to just sit by the fire with the TV off. Talk about your dreams and individual and couple goals. Stay in touch.

Most importantly, pray together as a couple. The spiritual unity that comes from praying together is powerful. Pray over each other, encourage each other and share your needs and disappointments. I have found that couples who stop praying together or don't do so at all have more problems than those who do pray together. Why? Because they tend to hide their distress and minimize the importance of spiritual unity. Spiritual unity builds intimacy. If you need to develop a more intimate bond with your spouse, begin a regular couple prayer time. You will be surprised what a difference it makes.

Turning Away From Each Other

Couples lock into negative cycles of interaction that often lead them apart. They turn away from each other rather than toward each other when stress mounts. Instead of forming a united front against stress and life pressures, the spouse becomes the enemy. This happened to Dan and Rita.

Dan and Rita were diagnosed with infertility. The specialists didn't know why the couple wasn't able to achieve pregnancy. It just wasn't happening. Months of testing, drugs, shots and procedures led to years of coping with the chronic stress of infertility. Rita hated her malfunctioning body, and Dan couldn't relieve the pressure of Rita's continued unhappiness. He too wanted a family. The ongoing stress of infertility led Dan and Rita to distance emotionally. Instead of supporting each other and growing stronger, they withdrew and became depressed.

The couple stopped talking. They came home from their jobs and wandered into different rooms of the house. During dinner, they read the newspaper and barely acknowledged the other. Rita's depression spiraled downward, and Dan wanted to be away from her as much as possible. Her daily crying was more than he could bear. He didn't know how to help her, for his own unhappiness was too great.

Instead of getting help to understand the incredible strain infertility presented, Dan and Rita drifted apart. They didn't use each other as a buffer against the stress. Instead, each became the victim of stress. Blame went unspoken but festered in their hearts.

As they started nitpicking each other, memories of their relationship began to change. The once positive couple began rewriting their history. Positive memories were replaced by more recent negative experiences until finally they believed things had always been terrible. Only moments of hurt stood out.

In truth, this couple, like most, started out on positive ground. Unfortunately, they got stuck in the pain and stress related to a chronic medical condition. Eventually they divorced.

Gottman's Relationship Killers

In the cases above, the couples behaved in ways that turned their relationships from positive to negative. Their exchanges became more negative until finally they developed contempt for each other. Feelings of contempt create emotional distance, which eventually leads to divorce.

It takes time and hard work to get to the point of feeling nothing toward your spouse. You don't wake up one day and say, "I don't love that person anymore." According to Gottman's research, relationship deterioration is progressive and involves at least four elements—criticism, contempt, defensiveness, and stonewalling.[2] These four responses are destructive to any relationship. Over time, they do great damage. They eventually lead to emotional distance—a major predictor of divorce. What Gottman may or may not know is that these four things also displease God.

Criticism

Everyone gets angry with a partner once in awhile. Everyone has disagreements. Anger, which, by the way, has a bad rap, is not an evil emotion, as we learned in chapter 6. Anger is a natural response to injustice. It's OK to have it. It's what you do with anger that counts. If you hold on to it, you create problems. When you insult the very being of your spouse, you are not only angry, but you are also critical.

For example, if your husband missed your son's birthday party because he stayed late at work, you'd be angry. Your husband's behavior hurt your son's feelings and yours. You can do one of three things with your anger:

1 Lash out and insult him: "You are a jerk who doesn't care about his son or wife."

2 Become critical at other times because you've stored up the anger. A month later when he forgets to bring in the mail, you can say, "All you ever do is think of yourself." This response would be "left-over" anger from the previous "meal" of injustice. You will have allowed resentment to build, which is expressed in angry put-downs.

3 Address the behavior you don't like: "Staying late made you miss the party. Now your son is upset. He wanted you here. So did I. It makes us both feel unimportant in your life. I'm angry, and so is he."

The last option simply addresses the problem that led to the angry feeling. The other two responses involve criticism. The goal of criticism is to put down the person, not deal with the issue. For example, "The way you file our bills is ridiculous. Only a moron files the way you do. I married a moron." This type of criticism wears on relationships because it tears at the very being of a person. Over time, criticism kills a relationship, especially when it is "dished out" more often than positive comments.

To tear down the fiber of a person is ungodly. We are to be encouragers, praying for and supporting one another, speaking kind and gentle words. When we criticize people for being who they are, we rip apart their sense of self.

I'm not saying you should stop confronting problems. But I am saying there is a good way and a not-so-good way to confront. Confronting the issue or the problem behavior is appropriate. Constructive criticism is helpful and sharpens us. (See Proverbs 27:17.) Slamming the other person, making fun of him or her or putting that person down is hurtful and wrong and warned about in Matthew 7:1–6.

Contempt

When you feel *contempt* for someone, you despise that person. Contempt goes beyond disapproval to downright disgust. If you begin to think about your partner this way, you are headed for divorce. There is a difference between *disapproval* of your partner's behavior and feelings of *contempt*.

You may start out disapproving specific actions. But when you allow that disapproval to grow and begin to attribute it to some "badness" in the other person, you reinforce feelings of contempt. Then any disapproving behavior becomes reinforcing evidence of why you disdain your partner.

In my experience, couples ready to divorce have allowed this feeling of contempt to grow and be reinforced in their thinking. Divorce becomes an option because they can't stand the other person. They no longer get angry or disappointed—now all they feel is contempt for their partner. The usual comment is, "I just don't love her anymore." Of course not; you've allowed contempt to enter the relationship. It kills off love.

Sue and Ryan felt contempt for one another. Marital therapy was virtually impossible because all they did was mock any attempt to repair their relationship. The homework assignments I gave to them were sabotaged by their cynicism and sarcastic remarks. One spouse began an assignment, and the other made fun of it. When I tried to deal with the couple, almost every exchange ended in hostility. They would not control their tongues and were masterful at name-calling, blaming and degrading each other.

So I began to see these two in individual sessions. Each had entrenched negative thoughts about the other. Until they were ready to address the contempt they felt, not much would change.

Probably one of the best examples of contempt between marital partners was shown in the 1989 movie *War of the Roses*. The story is about the demise of a couple's relationship after eighteen years of marriage. Their growing hatred for each other progresses to destructive proportions. Watching the characters played by Kathleen Turner and Michael Douglas is a painful experience played out by many couples. I didn't find this dark comedy funny, because it was a large-screen reminder of the hate that can breed in relationships.

When I read the Gospel accounts in which the Pharisees tried to trip up Jesus, I realize that contempt must have had deep roots in their hearts. They were always so angry with Him—He healed on the Sabbath, said He was God, saw through their religious acts, broke the rules by talking to the poor, women and the sick and touched dead people when He wasn't supposed to. Over time these upsetting acts turned into contempt for Jesus. How else could the Pharisees plot to kill Him?

We can be like Pharisees in our marriages. We get upset when our spouses don't do things the "right way." We find fault. Over time we allow that fault to move from criticism to contempt. Eventually we can't stand the person we married. We want a divorce.

Contempt has no place in the heart of a Christian. The injunction to love one another (the greatest commandment) precludes a place for contempt in our lives. We cannot allow anger and bitterness to fester. Contempt is the fruit of such seed. If you find yourself feeling contempt for your partner, there is a spiritual root that needs to be destroyed. Whatever led you to that point must be dealt with swiftly in love, forgiveness, release of judgment and grace.

Defensiveness

Defensiveness is a self-preservation response to relationship problems. It blocks intimacy and is not helpful. Defensiveness is usually motivated by fear and insecurity when you feel attacked. If your spouse is overly critical or on the attack, it is easy to become defensive. But if you stay defensive, your relationship suffers.

When you are defensive you don't hear the problem, you don't process information accurately, and you don't solve anything. You can't solve anything because you are too busy keeping up your guard. Defensiveness creates a wall. The wall blocks intimacy, and eventually couples grow emotionally apart. And remember, emotional distance is a significant predictor of divorce.

Defensive people are not usually open to change because they are too busy protecting themselves. Jeff and Julie refused to put down their guard to entertain ideas of reconciliation. They weren't willing to take the risk. In Jeff's words, "I don't want to try with Julie anymore. What if she hurts me again? I won't put myself in that position."

Too many couples stay in a defensive posture, afraid they will be hurt again. Sometimes the root of this is pride. Other times it is related to vulnerability. "I'm not letting down my guard because I might get slammed again." Yes, it's true, you might. But the alternative is to stay defensive and distant—which eventually leads to emotional withdrawal. The solution is to find someone who can help create a safe atmosphere in which you can discuss your problems. Your guard must be lowered for problems to be confronted. However, this needs to be done in a safe and healthy manner.

It's hard to be vulnerable and open when you've been hurt. That's where a trained marital therapist can help. There may need to be rules concerning how you talk to one another and someone to mediate your interactions. If you want to stop the negativity, you can. There is no excuse not to try unless you have an unwilling heart.

Stonewalling

Stonewalling is another emotional response to criticism and contempt. It too is a defensive posture. It happens when a spouse who is engaged in bitter criticism and feelings of contempt shuts down emotionally and refuses to respond. He or she tunes out. Jeff was stonewalling with Julie. He no longer wanted to be part of her life and didn't want to hear what she had to say. He emotionally disconnected from his wife. Usually this response comes after criticism, contempt and defensiveness have been present for a while.

Typically, men do more stonewalling than women. This has to do with the way men respond physically to arguments and upsets. It's true—there is a physiological gender difference to dealing with conflict.

When men and women fight, men become more physically distressed and stay that way longer. Physically, fighting feels lousy to men, which is why they tend to avoid it. And they stay upset longer after the fight is over.[3]

Typically, women don't like stonewalling. They become very upset with this response. They react emotionally to shut down and are often called "hysterical, overreactive or too emotional." Men go into their "feel-nothing state" and try to escape because of the unpleasant physical reactions strife brings to their bodies.

Gottman's research shows that during an argument, men become more physiologically distressed—higher blood pressure and heart rate. They have what researchers call a *higher arousal*. A way to reduce arousal is to back off, retreat, become silent or, over time, stonewall.

Women don't have this same level of arousal. Consequently women will "go after" a fight and are often the pursuers in relationship difficulties. The complaint of many wives is that they are tired "of beating their head against a *stone wall*." But women also suffer physically from unhappy marriages.

In healthy marriages men are expressive. Contrary to popular belief, men are quite capable of sharing feelings. Some men may be conflict avoiders but don't detach from the emotional relationship.

Stonewallers detach. They detach because they don't want to become flooded with negativity that physiologically arouses them. Emotionally they hang on to negative thoughts about their partner. Stonewalling is the ultimate defense shield. It protects from emotional distress.

If you are at war with your partner, beware. Not only will it kill your relationship, but it could also damage your physical health. A marriage based on hostile and distant reactions to a spouse may actually suppress the immune system and make you more susceptible to physical illness.[4]

Growing Apart

Take the case of Dustin and Ann. They have nothing good to say about each other. All that comes out of their mouths is defensiveness and mutual contempt. It doesn't matter what subject is brought up, the result is always the same— war. They are trapped in a cycle of negative exchange. When they speak to each other, their muscles are tense, their hearts beat faster, and they can't breathe. Their inability to soothe each other places them in physical danger.

Ann is more likely to complain, criticize and make demands on Dustin. She wants a reaction from him. Dustin tends to rationalize, avoid and withdraw. He becomes more physically aroused during a fight than Ann. He wants to avoid those unpleasant feelings of arousal. Ann tolerates emotional arousal. Not only is this couple in danger of divorce, but the marriage is taking a physical toll on both, even though they react differently to problems. Dustin doesn't like being physically aroused by all the negativity. His way of coping is to check out, to distance himself emotionally from Ann's constant complaints. Ann's anger increases because of his distancing behavior. She goes after him. The more she does, the more Dustin withdraws. Over time, his avoidance comes with a physical price.

Ann is physically ill over the marital problems. For years, she has beaten her head against Dustin's stone wall. She keeps trying to get a response from Dustin despite his obvious distancing from her. She is at risk. Research actually shows that by counting the number of Dustin's facial expressions of contempt for Ann, she could estimate the number of infectious diseases she might contract over the next four years![5]

Dustin and Ann are unable to soothe one another because of the cycle of contempt, distance and pursuit. Their relationship is characterized by hostile and negative exchanges with no evidence of being able to repair the damage they inflict on one another. Incredibly unhappy, physically at risk–should we give up on Ann and Dustin?

Dustin and Ann need to stop inflicting pain on each other. Each suffers physical side effects from their unhappy marriage. They don't listen to each other or a therapist because they are so physiologically aroused. Their emotions overtake them. They are distressed and in need of help.

They need self-control. Dustin and Ann are so busy hanging on to injury or planning the next evasive tactic that they don't consider the "rightfulness" of their responses. Are they evidencing the fruit of the Spirit through complaint, criticism and demand? Is emotional avoidance God's way to deal with a spouse?

We are supposed to guard our tongues. When we resort to criticism and demand, we are hardly showing Christ's love to our partner. When we avoid conflict or emotional exchange, we are not resolving issues.

So how do we begin to turn the tide in what looks like a surefire divorce situation? Gottman developed a technique to help couples change highly negative interactions. He advises that both spouses be trained in soothing skills to help them calm down. Calming down lessens physical arousal and makes it more possible to hear the other and be less toxic.

He suggests that when you have a difficult interaction, you monitor your heart rate. If your heart rate increases ten beats per minute over its regular rate, stop the interaction. Take a break (at least twenty minutes) and do something soothing. During this time do NOT think about the faults of your partner. Instead, calm yourself (a walk, music, counting to ten, prayer).[6]

Better yet, take the biblical advice and think on thoughts that are noble, of good report or positive about your partner (Phil. 4:8). They may not come to mind immediately, but force yourself to remember a positive moment. Your body will calm down. Then you can hear and deal better with your partner. When you are overloaded by emotion, you can't think clearly, and no amount of therapy helps.

Next, give your spouse the benefit of the doubt. Try this: *He's only saying this because he's mad. He loves me and really doesn't want to hurt me.* As you calm down, listen and validate what your spouse is saying.

When you become successful at calming down, try adding words of affection toward your spouse. For example, "Honey, we are going to find a way to work this out because we love each other." Or, "I love you and don't want to fight like this."

Spiritually, you are practicing self-control. You choose to think on good things, to calm down your body and to try to listen to your spouse. Not only will you have fewer health problems, but you'll also be acting according to the instructions God has given. Jesus is less concerned about how "right" we are and more concerned about how we treat the other.

Understanding Passion

Couples also complain about loss of sexual interest. Usually it is the wife who reports low or no sexual desire, although men have this complaint as well. Both husband and wife may feel passion is gone. Frustrated and even ashamed, they are bewildered as to how their passion dwindled to almost nothing. The immediate assumption is that something terrible is wrong in the relationship. There must be a deep hidden emotional problem that only Freud could understand!

In many cases, relationship issues are the key to unlocking lost passion and renewing sexual interest. When you are constantly criticized or belittled, it is hard to feel passionate toward that person. If contempt has set in, the last thing on your mind is a meaningful sexual encounter. But for some couples, understanding the biology of desire helps. It's possible to be deeply in love with your spouse and have low sexual desire. Don't confuse your lack of desire with lost love. Here's why.

Desire differences are normal. Relationships usually begin with intense passion. Initially, you overlook the fact that he can't make a move without consulting his mother, or that she really is obsessed with shopping. After all, you are in love. Initial passion or infatuation does burn intensely because of the neurochemistry behind it. According to experts, infatuation lasts about eighteen to thirty-six months for most couples. Your hidden biology is thought to be the cause.[7]

Although the theory is based on animal studies, research psychiatrist Michael Liebowitz at New York State Psychiatric Institute believes biochemical attraction goes this way: We meet someone to whom we are attracted. That attraction causes our brains to become saturated with certain neurotransmitters that stimulate desire. We call this romantic love.[8]

What couples often fail to understand is that the burning fire of passion eventually simmers. This cool down, if not understood, may leave one feeling disillusioned and distressed.

Hormones play a role. Take testosterone, for example. This steroid hormone produced by both sexes correlates strongly with desire. After initial infatuation burns off, a low-testosterone woman can feel sexually disinterested.

Men, on the other hand, have ten times the testosterone levels as women. (Women have lower amounts but are more sensitive to the hormone.) Their "T" (testosterone) levels drop gradually with age but are genetically determined by the sensitivity of androgen receptors in the genitals. Typically, men have stronger desire than women. Of course, there are exceptions to this rule.[9]

As mentioned above, during the time of infatuation, neurotransmitter release in the brain is time-limited. This means the chemical "love cocktail" eventually wears off. For some people, their normal sexual desire is masked at the beginning of a relationship because of initial infatuation. Afterward, testosterone levels play an important part in ongoing desire. If you are a high T person married to a low T, you may have problems. Why? Because a high T desires sex more often than a low T. Low T people begin to question their love for their spouses. They also blame themselves for lack of desire.

Thus, sometimes lack of sexual desire can be related to hormones. Instead of just assuming your relationship is deeply troubled, consider the role biochemistry may play. *All* low desire isn't a result of relationship problems or deep intrapsychic issues.

No matter what the cause, most of us have to work on sustaining sexual intimacy in marriage. But remember this: Passion is time-limited; sexual desire may be related to biochemical factors; and sustaining sexual interest includes physical as well as relationship factors.

The point of this brief discussion about the role of biochemistry is simply this: Don't always assume that the lack of passion is strictly relationship based. In most cases, relationship factors play a major role. But in some cases, hormones may be involved. Remember to consider your physiology before you determine lost passion is related to lost love.

Rid Yourself of Negativity

Let's recap. You need the five-to-one rule operational in your relationship, which means you must get rid of criticism, contempt, defensiveness and stonewalling. So how do you do this without spending your life in therapy?

1. Remember your history.

Most likely, you and your spouse started out as friends. Try to remember this when things get tense. How would you treat your best friend if you started having relationship problems? Hopefully not by being critical and defensive. What attracted you to each other? What made you fall in love? How were the two of you behaving when the relationship was strong? Reminisce. Rehearse the terrific moments of the relationship.

2. Talk about positive moments in your relationship.

Purposefully identify the good qualities about your partner and speak them aloud. Then build on those moments with caring, kind and considerate behavior and speech. Don't wait for your spouse to do this first, and don't gauge your reaction based on what he or she does. You determine to line up your tongue and thoughts according to God's Word. As you daily praise God, praise your partner. Keep your thoughts focused on what God can do. In an act of faith, believe God will turn your relationship around. Start the process with positive talk. Guard your tongue and mind. You have more power to change your own perceptions of your partner than you realize.

3. Build caring behavior into the relationship.

There is an old exercise therapists give to marital couples called "caring days." In this exercise developed by Richard Stuart, each spouse writes a list of things that would make him or her feel good. The things are very specific, like, "Kiss me when you come home from work." "Tell me you love me every day." "Help with the children's baths." They trade lists, and the other spouse is asked to do as many things on the list each day as possible. The purpose of this exercise is to help couples define and restore caring moments to the relationship.

4. Love your spouse as yourself.

This is a guiding principle for all relationships—love your spouse as yourself. If you don't love yourself, work on that first. Find out what God has to say about you and what blocks you from a positive view of self. Learn to see yourself as God sees you—wonderfully made, blessed, redeemed and loved. For example:

- ⊙⊙ God loves you as you are (John 3:16).

- ⊙⊙ You are a new creature (2 Cor. 5:17).

- ⊙⊙ You are God's child (John 1:12).

- ⊙⊙ You are the temple of God, and His Spirit dwells within you (1 Cor. 3:16).

- ⊙⊙ You are constantly on God's mind (Ps. 139:2).

- ⊙⊙ You are free (John 8:36).

- ⊙⊙ You have the mind of God (1 Cor. 2:16).

Review all the biblical descriptions given about your identity. There are many in the Bible. Some of you may need counseling to help with this process. Then love your spouse with God's love. He loves you unconditionally. Do the same for your spouse.

5. Understand the sowing and reaping principle.

What we sow we reap (Gal. 6:7). As long as the earth remains, there will be seed time and harvest. That's another foundational principle. If you sow words of hurt, insult and harm, you'll eventually reap them as well. Does that mean your marriage will break up? Maybe not, but you will feel the repercussion of this behavior somewhere in your life because God's principles work every time.

The best thing is to sow good seeds of kindness, gentleness, love, patience, faithfulness, goodness, joy, kindness, longsuffering, peace, self-control—all the fruit of the Spirit. You will reap a good relationship harvest from these seeds.

If you don't deal with conflicts, over a period of time bad feelings may build up. Enter the four relationship bad guys—criticism, contempt, defensiveness and stonewalling. God tells us not to have a critical spirit, not to feel contempt toward anyone and to solve our differences. When we are disobedient to God, we open the door for problems.

How do you sow wisely? You plant good seed (the Word) into your heart. Out of the heart grows love. Love, according to 1 Corinthians 13, is patient, slow to anger, kind, gentle, giving, truthful, honest, hopeful, encouraging and endures to the end. It isn't rude or provoking. The love of God, to us and through us, behaves as described.

6. Understand the power of the tongue.

The Bible is clear about the power of the tongue. Read James 3, and you will learn how the tongue guides your entire body. According to James, the tongue reveals what is in the heart, and it can cause great damage. We are instructed to get control of it, which includes not letting it run rampant against our spouse. Words, as you know, can create deep wounds. We can't praise God and then verbally blast away at our partner.

It is clear that the confession of your mouth is powerful. Proverbs 25:15 says, "A gentle tongue breaks a bone," meaning that a rebuke given in love is valuable. James 1:26 says that if we think we are religious but don't control our tongue, we deceive our heart. Get control of your tongue, and your marriage will improve. Again, self-control results from love—the first fruit of the Spirit.

So how do you get control over your tongue? Say what God says about you and your partner. This may require faith, but when your partner does something hurtful, don't lash out with the tongue. Speak the truth in love, correct in love if necessary, but don't demolish the person with your words. You can't do that in love.

The battle to bring a marriage back from emotional distance is fierce because it requires submission to several spiritual principles. Many of us don't want to submit to what

God says about the tongue, behavior and love. It's hard work to conform to the image of Christ, and we feel our flesh pull us to behave other ways. But if you want to divorce-proof your marriage, you need to get control of your tongue and not allow these relationship killers to permeate your marriage. As you learn to control the tongue and concentrate on praise, your feelings toward your partner change. Like the old parenting adage says, "Catch them being good." In this case apply it to your children *and* your spouse.

Don't allow criticism to creep into the relationship. At the first sign of it, get help. If you feel contempt for anyone, something is wrong. You may need to extend grace, forgive and let go of injustice. But don't stay in contempt. You can't feel contempt toward your spouse and please God. It's impossible!

Review

Lie #5 *I've lost that loving feeling, and it's gone, gone, gone!*

Truth #5 *That loving feeling can be restored.*

Divorce-Proofing Strategies

- Put the five-to-one rule to work in your relationship (five positives for every negative).

- Lose criticism, contempt, defensiveness and stonewalling, and replace them with godly love for others and yourself.

- Support each other during times of stress—do not distance.

- Maintain friendship with your spouse.

- Review your positive history together, and reinforce those memories.

- Love your spouse as yourself. (You may first have to learn to love yourself.)

- Remember the principle of sowing and reaping.

- Know the cause for lack of desire. Is it relationship based or hormonally driven?

Growing Apart

- Take control of your tongue and thoughts.
- Build caring behavior into your daily relationship.
- Begin a couple prayer time together.

CHAPTER 8

Gender Relations

Lie #6

A more traditional marriage will save us.

Forget *Star Wars;* we have *Gender Wars* playing at a couple's home near you:

He's too dominating.
She should submit.

He wants dinner on the table when he walks in the door.
She shouldn't work outside the home.

He should help out with the kids.
She's been home all day. What's she been doing?

He treats me like a child.
She acts like I'm her dad.

He controls the money.
She can have money whenever she asks for it.

Let's face it. We all have long lists of how our partner should behave. Our lists are influenced by how we think about gender roles. Gender ideas come from the culture, our families and our personal experiences with men and women. What is usually missing is an informed biblical view.

Gender is a hot button for most couples. Arguments can be traced to core assumptions each partner has about how men and women are supposed to relate. Yet these assumptions are rarely discussed prior to marriage, so they play out in any number of ways. For example, should husbands help out in the kitchen? Should wives run family finances? The answers to questions like these depend on your personal views about gender.

Trouble erupts when we have different ideas about how men and women should behave. Fights can even lead to divorce when couples don't know how to balance power and treat each other with mutual respect. If you want to divorce-proof your marriage, tackle the gender issues in your relationship. Make gender a topic of discussion. Then check to see if there is hidden anger over gender disagreements.

Gender issues involve the use and abuse of power. The sobering truth (borne out by research) is that marriage is not always good for women. Married women have higher incidences of emotional and physical health problems compared to unmarried women. The opposite is true for men. Married men live longer, suffer less depression and are healthier than unmarried men.[1] And for some women, marriage is a private hell of abuse.

A Problem With Submission?

Jerry: "Dr. Mintle, you are a Christian woman. Teach my wife how to be a properly submissive wife. We wouldn't fight if she would just let me lead. Someone's filled her head with feminism, and I can't deal with her. All we do is argue lately.

She won't listen to me or do what I tell her. It's not like I'm not good to her. I give her money when she needs it. I tell her she's a good housewife. I don't get it."

Shauna: "He *doesn't* get it. He's living in the 1950s and keeps talking about having a 'traditional' family. He wants me to do everything at home and never question his decisions. I lived on my own for five years before we married and did well, thank you. He treats me like I don't have a brain in my head and keeps quoting Scripture about women submitting to their husbands. People at church tell me to do what he says and not question him. It's my godly duty. Somehow, this doesn't feel very godly. Would God give me a brain and then not expect me to use it? And since when am I not allowed to question my husband's decisions? We are supposed to be a team, not a dictatorship.

"I like to work, and I hate housework. I don't want to stay home all day. I had a job when I met Jerry. It didn't seem to bother him when we dated. Now all of a sudden he wants me to quit my job and stay home. To do what? He thinks our marriage will improve. It won't. I'll get depressed!"

Jerry and Shauna are at an impasse over gender roles and expectations. Jerry's view of a woman's role doesn't match Shauna's. Both admit they never talked about these issues prior to marriage. Now, their different views are causing problems.

Jerry wants his wife to behave like Mrs. Brady of television's *The Brady Bunch*. Jerry had a domineering father who controlled his mother. His mother was never allowed to give an opinion or make a decision. Jerry's only husband model was his dad. Husbands make decisions, and wives agree to them. What was Shauna's problem? Jerry admitted he never studied the Bible, but he knew the passage that says, "Wives, submit to your husbands." He quotes it whenever Shauna disagrees with him.

Shauna was raised by a single mother whose husband

walked away from the family when Shauna was a baby. She, like many Americans, didn't come from a "traditional" family. Her mom worked to support the children. Shauna is like her mom—determined, smart and intuitive—all qualities that were attractive to Jerry.

Shauna has been deferring to Jerry because he insists this is God's way. She hasn't read much of the Bible either. She is uncertain what it means to be a Christian wife. She just knows that staying home won't solve her marital problems. Resentment would skyrocket. The people at church seem to side with Jerry, and she feels guilty, as if she's doing something wrong.

The couple asked for help at their church. An older couple told them that men lead and women follow. Shauna should submit to Jerry no matter what. If Jerry wants her to quit her job, he must have a good reason.

Shauna feels she has submitted beyond what is reasonable and that Jerry uses the submission argument whenever he doesn't get his way. She wants to be involved in decisions and treated with respect. She doesn't want to quit her job. She has been promoted twice in six months. Lately Jerry's been asking about the men with whom she works.

Jerry's marital problems are not about whether or not Shauna works. The bigger issue is the way Jerry tries to control his wife and overpower the relationship. Relationships involve power. How that power is managed and shared is crucial. Jerry worries that Shauna will meet someone on the job and leave him. Several of his coworkers have had affairs. He fears Shauna will have an affair because she is around men at work. He doesn't trust her to control herself, even though she has never given him cause to worry. In reality, Jerry struggles with his own sexual impulses and projects his insecurities onto Shauna.

The couple who counseled with them at church needs a better understanding of submission. To tell a woman to submit blindly to her husband's demands is foolish. That is not what godly submission is all about.

Furthermore, what Christians often cite as the normative or traditional family is a more recent cultural by-product of urbanization, industrialization and individual trends over the past two centuries. Yes, the nuclear family was around long before industrial America, but it was different in its form—home was a place of living and working together in which all family members shared responsibility. People married for practical—not romantic—reasons. And traditional homes were not free of abuse and incest.

The nuclear family with father as breadwinner and mother as homemaker, mother and child-rearer is a product of the twentieth century and the urban middle class. In the post–World War II explosion of suburban life (witness the now famous "baby boom") Americans moved toward the "Beaver Cleaver" lifestyle. Now Christians tend to romanticize the traditional family as the ideal for every family. When marital problems arise, the assumption is that the more traditional the family becomes, the stronger the marriage will be. Nowhere in the Bible does God elevate middle-class American homes in the 1950s as the standard for successful families.

Now before you rise up in arms and dismiss me as some wild feminist railing against men and the church, read on. I'm not going to propose anything anti-biblical. In fact, I'm going to outline what I believe the Bible says about gender relations. If you have a traditional marriage relationship and things are going well—great! Who am I to tell you to stop doing what's working? If both of you are happy with the arrangement, carry on. But for those of you who are unhappy and still fighting gender wars, you need to know the biblical rules.

In their effort to help Jerry and Shauna, the couple who counseled with them at church unintentionally cemented the wrongly assumed impasses and further alienated Shauna.

She, like many Christian women, lives between a rock and a hard place—wanting to do the right biblical thing, but feeling guilty because she doesn't understand what that is and how it's supposed to work. Intuitively she knows God didn't create her with gifts and talents she should never use. God, who loves men and women equally, can't possibly expect her to be a mindless robot under Jerry's control.

Biblical submission is not about going brain dead under the power and control of a husband—or a wife for that matter. Jerry needs Shauna's input. It would greatly relieve the pressure on him caused by having to make all decisions alone. This couple needs a better understanding of God's plan for their equality.

Truth #6

God's intention is gender equality.

S ocial change has led to confusion. Society says one thing. The church says another. Within the church, views vary from conservative to liberal. How are men and women supposed to relate in marriage? Is returning to the way things were fifty years ago the solution for troubled marriages? Hardly.

A core tenet of feminism is that men and women are equally qualified and entitled to participate fully in the human experience. Feminists are actually on to something here. Unwittingly, they understand what God originally intended for the sexes. They just don't recognize that the way to accomplish this goal is through the power of Jesus Christ. Gender reconciliation requires an understanding of God's plan and a transformed life.

We Live After the Fall—Not Before It

The reason we need transformation is because we live *after* the Fall. Let's backtrack. Because we were created in God's image, both sexes have equal worth. One is not better than the other. In marriage we are covenant partners imaged after God.

Before the Fall there is no mention in the Bible of man ruling over woman. They shared dominion over the Earth and had immediate access to God.

It is often argued that because woman was created as "helper," she was designed to be subordinate to man. But Bible scholars tell us that the Hebrew word for *helper, ezer,* does not mean second-class or inferior. It means "suitable for him" or "corresponding to him," which implies equality. And after creating them male and female, God blesses both.

Prior to Adam and Eve's disobedience, each was dependent on God for everything. They walked and talked with God daily in the Garden. Their sin moved them from godly dependence to independence. Their disobedience caused them to become fearful. Then God cursed the serpent, condemning it to a belly-in-the-dust existence and an eternal mortal struggle with man.

God did not curse man and woman, but He condemned them to afflictions. The price of independence was huge. Sin changed who man and woman were intended to be. A major consequence was the subordination of women and dominance of men. The Fall in Eden disrupted God's perfect plan for mankind, and it effected the destruction of His perfect plan for the sexes.

Since we live after the Fall, we too are affected by that gender fallout. Certainly the Old Testament is filled with rape, lust, seduction, adultery, sexual sin, polygamy, incest, domination and subordination. This same fallen nature of humankind too often shows up in marriage.

Jesus, the Model of Gender Restoration

But God sent Jesus so that sin would not prevail among humankind. Jesus came to redeem us from the Fall through the forgiveness of sins. Equal to the Father, He submitted to the Father and was obedient unto death. The fact that Jesus submitted to God was important—that is our model. Submit first to God, then to each other.

By choosing submission, Jesus transformed social relationships. He redeemed the spiritual condition of male and female. In Christ there is no racial, social, economic or gender discrimination—there is no Jew or Greek, no slave or free, no male or female (Gal. 3:28). Our differences do not matter in Christ.

What can we learn from Jesus, our model of reconciliation and conformity? According to Philip Yancey in *The Jesus I Never Knew*, He . . .

- Was compassionate to the ill.

- Was intolerant of injustice.

- Elevated the status of women.

- Did not support the male structure of superiority and privilege of the day.

- Did not fit the traditional masculine stereotype of the culture. He incorporated masculine and feminine traits into His personhood.

- Praised Mary of Bethany for choosing to listen to Him instead of serving a meal.

- Told the Samaritan woman (an outsider) He was the Messiah.

- Had women travel with Him and the disciples.

- Appeared first to Mary and told her to be His witness after the Resurrection.

- Confronted the men who wanted to stone the adulterous woman for hypocrisy.

- Stood for monogamy even though Jews were permitted polygamy under law.

- Gave the same rights and privileges to husbands and wives.

- Hung out with men and women of low socioeconomic status.

- Showed a wide range of emotions that today are labeled more typically feminine—joy, meekness, sadness (He cried), compassion, love.

Jesus radicalized the social structure of the day. He spoke of equality and lived it. He restored gender relations. He resisted the oppression of women, the poor and discrimination based on race or ethnicity. If we are to be like Him, we need to do the same.[2]

The Fall resulted in man's sin tendency to abuse his authority and assume power *over* women. For women, the tendency is to disrespect a man's role of leadership, to lack self-affirmation and to be afraid of power. Men must guard against a tendency to overpower, criticize and disrespect women. Women must not be afraid of who they are in Christ. Christian men and women are to counteract sin with the gospel of Christ.

The model of Christ on earth was servant headship. He submitted to His Father in a loving servant manner. His death was the ultimate expression of submitting His will to the will of the Father.

Submit to God, Then to Each Other

Men and women are to be equally submitted in love to one another. When this happens, men don't dominate and women don't resist. Instead, a godly model emerges of working side by side as co-companions with mutual respect. First submit to God's plan, then submit to each other.

The problem I see in most marriages is an unwillingness to submit to God's plan. Men who take power and abuse it are outside God's plan. Women who don't exercise their own spiritual priesthood but depend on men to blindly lead them do not understand Scripture. What I usually see in therapy are dependent women angry at controlling men. Neither is godly.

Lose Your Gender Stereotype

This doesn't mean men and women don't have different roles and functions. Men and women are different. Roles and functions need to be negotiated in marriage. Power distribution should be agreed upon. This is a core issue for most marriages.

Power imbalances create conflicts that often lead to divorce. Yes, feminists are for equal power, but the way you acquire, use and define that power is important. Your personal character and the way you relate to another person must always be conformed to Christ—not to some other standard.

Paul speaks about the Christian temperament in Galatians 5:22–23: "But the fruit of the Spirit is love, joy, peace, long-suffering, kindness, goodness, faithfulness, gentleness, self-control"—character traits considered to be mostly feminine in today's culture.

Jesus embodied both male and female character traits. Today, though, we have segregated those traits. Both genders need to be liberated from culturally assigned gender boxes. Couples must clarify role expectations and not lord power over one another. Mutual respect and affirmation are needed.

Gender Relations

Alongside the biblical mandates of gender relations, what does the marital research offer us? You may be surprised to learn that it actually supports a biblical view of gender relations.

Listen to the Queen of Soul—R-E-S-P-E-C-T

According to research by Gottman and colleagues, most stable marriages have a husband and wife who treat each other with respect and allow mutual influence.[3] In healthy marriages, men don't resist sharing power, decision-making or accepting a wife's influence. Because there is mutual respect when problems arise, compromise is easier. Collaboration and consent replace coercion and control.

Gottman studied newlyweds to see how they handled conflict. An interesting gender difference was observed. During arguments, women expressed some negative emotions but generally didn't escalate the fights. They tended to match the husband's level of intensity. But husbands who became critical or defensive and would not accept their wives' influence did escalate conflict. This led to marital instability.

In our culture women more easily accept the influence of men. However, when men don't accept the influence of women, the marriage is at risk. Men who will not share power with women are four times more likely to divorce or live in unhappy marriages.[4]

The bottom line of Gottman's research is that mutual respect and honor keep a marriage healthy. These two qualities are also hallmarks of strong friendships. So to divorce-proof your marriage, build a strong friendship based on mutual honor and respect.

Two Skills to Balance Power

Since the use and abuse of power are such critical issues in divorce-proofing, there are two skills couples must develop to work effectively on power imbalances: empowerment and empathy. Let's take a look at each.

Empowerment

If you have been married for any length of time you know it's impossible to share every task and responsibility equally. You each have different skills and abilities. However, one goal of marriage is to empower your spouse. *Empowerment* means establishing power in the other. The way you do this is to recognize the strengths your spouse brought into the marriage and encourage him or her to use these skills. Urge your spouse to become all he or she can become. Where there is a weak area in your spouse, work to strengthen it rather than tearing it down. The goal is for two people to empower each other to live up to their full potential.

In our culture, power is a precious commodity. More power means more influence. When Jesus came to earth, He did not use His power for personal benefit. Instead, He used His power to serve and lift up others, to forgive, to enable and to encourage. He is our model for empowerment. In marriage, we lift up our spouse, encourage him or her, forgive and enable emotional and spiritual health.

God's model of power is about equal access and equal opportunity. His resources are inexhaustible. Knowing this, we don't need to struggle for more of God's power just for ourselves. There is an abundance for everyone. So encourage your spouse to tap in to that continuous flow.

Unfortunately, empowering others takes a conscious effort. It's far easier to take control and misuse power because of our insecurities and mistrust. Every couple struggles with these issues and eventually must come to terms on power distribution within their marriage.

Empathy

Former President Bill Clinton won the hearts of so many

American women early on in his presidency because he "felt their pain." *Empathy* is about putting yourself in the shoes of someone else, understanding their issues from their point of view.

Couples need to address power issues by "feeling each other's pain." Because we are so different and come from different experiences, we need empathy. We often lack it because we're unaware of the experiences of others, or we prematurely attempt to solve problems before understanding all the elements of the problem, or because we have negative expectations for our spouse.

Women generally believe men lack empathy. Some do, but men are just as capable of empathy as women. The difference is that men often must be motivated to use it.[5]

Empathy between men and women is often lacking because of the way men and women think. For example, wives want husbands to listen. Men feel they show empathy by giving solutions. Take Jack and Jill. Jack tries to solve Jill's problem, thinking he is really helping. Jill wants to solve her own problem and is disturbed that Jack is telling her what to do. Both are upset and complain that the other has no empathy for the situation.

Jack and Jill must define what it is they expect from each other and what is helpful. She says, "Listen, hold my hand and give me eye contact, then I know you care. Let me try to solve the problem before you jump in with advice." Jack is relieved because he doesn't always have an answer. But he wants action to follow listening. He may have useful ideas, but he knows he married a competent woman.

Jack wants Jill to know, "Because I don't say much about feelings doesn't mean I don't have them. Give me time to think about what's going on, and don't jump all over me for not immediately sharing. I'm not as quick as you are when it comes to processing how I feel. So don't assume I don't ever feel. Sometimes I just need time to think about it."

In addition to defining what you want, couples must realize that men have been raised as men and women as women. As obvious as this statement is, it means we come from different gender biases. We need to appreciate these differences and work through them. Couples who share their gender experiences and feel listened to, do well together.

Marital Hot Spots

Now let's get more specific. What are the marital hot spots that gender affects? Start with this list, answering each of the questions:

1. Self-esteem

Do you make jokes about the opposite sex? Are they a put-down of men or women? Do you allow demeaning gender statements to come out of your mouth or laugh at the jokes of others? Do you ignore sexual harassment or, worse, participate in it? What message does this send to your spouse?

Obviously, you are not promoting gender respect. This kind of behavior hurts the self-esteem of a partner. A woman who harbors anger against men and makes digs at her husband is being disrespectful. Men who treat women as sexual objects and less than equals do the same.

2. Abuse of power—domestic violence

Do you physically abuse power? Do you intimidate through threats of violence?

I can't think of any way that distorts power more grossly between men and women than domestic violence. Domestic violence is an abuse of power—and it is sinful. There is no excuse for this behavior. Anyone who hits, beats and/or terrorizes another human being sins. Nothing justifies this response. No amount of marital tension gives either gender the right to hit or threaten. If there is domestic violence in your home, get help immediately. Someone is out of line and needs immediate correction.

3. Sex and intimacy

Do you use sex and intimacy as power issues?

Typically, women want emotional closeness before sex. Men, on the other hand, use sex to become emotionally close. This difference can set up a host of power issues that get acted out in other arenas of the marriage.

Have a conversation about your sexual life. Is it meeting the needs of each of you? Is it what you expect? Does either partner feel coerced or pressured for sex? What role does society play in your expectations of each other? Is there romance, sexual interest? If not, what is blocking these two things? How do you express intimacy? How would you like it expressed?

Pornography affects sex and intimacy in a negative way. It is based on images of women subjugated to men in demeaning ways through coercion and control. There is no place for such distortion of gender relations in the body of Christ. Despite what you may have heard, pornography does not help marriages. It does not improve your sex life and should not be used as a tool to do so. Get rid of it now!

4. Housework

Is housework only for women?

Rev up the vacuum cleaner. Pull out the dust cloth and get to work, men. You'll have a happier, less lonely and more involved marriage than your buddies who don't help around the house. Housewives all over America are applauding this finding. Finally, research that makes sense. Does it sound too good to be true?

Marital researcher John Gottman studied men who did housework and found them not only happier in their marriages, but they also have lower rates of heart disease and better health overall. In fact, these men were less stressed and less likely to be sick in the four years following their initial research meeting.[6]

I wish I could tell you that housework has curative powers—that doing housework is the key to fabulous relationships. This certainly would liberate a lot of women and encourage men to share in the exciting work of cleaning, but it isn't housework that cures troubled marriages. But for a moment, let's pretend it is. OK, back to reality.

Even though doing housework was tested as a separate factor in the marital study, housework really wasn't the issue. Actually, the husband who does housework tends to be a mutual and supportive partner. You see, spouses who act in mutual and supportive ways have good marriages. They also enjoy the physical benefits.

Men, the next time you see your wives struggle to keep up with all the housework, turn off the game, pull out that toilet bowl cleaner, pat yourselves on the back and say, "I'll be less lonely, less stressed and less likely to be sick if I scrub this commode." Your wives will give you a big smile (and maybe more), and say, "I'm glad I married that man!"

5. Show me the money

Does the one with the biggest portfolio get to be boss?

Couples fight most about money. Money is a source of power and influence. Typically men earn more of it than women. Personal power in marriage is often associated with how much money you bring to the relationship. In most cases, the more money a spouse brings in, the more they want in on what happens to it. Usually this means women are in a one-down position.

Potential abuse comes when men who earn more money decide that it entitles them to make unilateral decisions about expenditures. In these cases, money becomes a power club held threateningly over women's heads.

Many bright and capable women choose to stay in the dark about family finances (particularly stocks and investment portfolios), and consequently they don't contribute to money matters. Likewise, some men don't want to be investment lone rangers; they want input. They may worry that if something tragic were to happen to them, their wife wouldn't know what to do.

Decisions about how money is spent can become a power struggle. An impulse buyer, or conversely a penny pincher, can create tension in a marriage. Do you save, spend, buy now or pay with credit? What do you believe about men and women when it comes to working for pay?

I've had couples come to therapy because the wife makes more money than the husband—somehow they felt that wasn't right. The list of couple problems around money is long. The question to ask each other is, "What do we believe about gender and money?" Should women be at home, in the work force, earn the same as men, supervise men and so on. Your beliefs will create tension if they don't match your partner's and aren't worked out on a practical level.

6. Raising children

How are we going to split up the responsibilities?

Even though many couples believe moms and dads should be involved in the raising of children, this doesn't bear out in reality. We still have absentee and deadbeat dads, workaholics who rarely see their children, much less spend time with them, and moms trying to do the job of two parents. When there is an intact family, couples fight over mundane things like who will give the baby a bath, who will run to the store for groceries and whose job description trash falls under.

Bottom line—what roles are moms and dads supposed to occupy when it comes to raising kids? It all must be negotiated. Couples have to be flexible and adaptable or problems will continue.

I can't adequately address all the areas of power struggles between men and women in this short chapter. But I can tell you to begin talking about how gender influences your relationship based on what you've read so far.

I can also tell you that the power struggles won't get resolved by trying to revert to some idea about the good old days when men were men and women couldn't vote! Understand how your spouse thinks about gender issues, and be flexible when it comes to finding a workable arrangement. What works for one couple may not work for you. Therefore, the negotiation over who does what to whom needs much dialogue. What you *shouldn't* do is throw a few isolated scriptures at your partner and demand submission.

Go for What God Intended

If you study God's plan, you will find two occasions when He revealed His will on earth concerning gender—in the Garden and in the life of Christ. Look to those examples of how men and women should interact. You will find that no matter how you negotiate gender in your relationship, it must include mutual submission, respect, honor, empowerment and empathy. If you live your life by acting out those qualities, chances are you'll not abuse power in your relationship. You won't look at the good old days for current solutions. You'll look to God.

Review

Lie #6   *A more traditional marriage will save us.*

Truth #6   *God's intention is gender equality.*

Divorce-Proofing Strategies

- Submit first to God, then to each other.

- Define your gender expectations.

- Negotiate roles and tasks so that both spouses are in agreement.

- Build a strong friendship with your spouse based on respect and honor.

- Empower your spouse.

- Develop empathy for your spouse.

- Address marital hot spots of power imbalances: self-esteem, domestic violence, sex and intimacy, housework, money and raising children.

- God's will for gender relationships is revealed twice on Earth—in the Garden of Eden and in Christ when He walked on Earth. Look to those examples to pattern your relationships.

CHAPTER 9

Power Outage

Lie #7

I can't change—this is who I am;
take it or leave it.

I can't change. This is who I am. Take it or leave it. Someone else will accept me for me." Have you or someone you know used this excuse when it comes to marital trouble? It's a lame excuse, and I have never understood why people tell me this. I'm a therapist! My goal is to help people change. If change weren't possible, I'd be out of a job.

Let's not forget that change is the hallmark of Christian conversion. When you asked Christ into your life, you were immediately transformed to a new creation. *New* is the operative word here. *New* implies a change from the *old* way you thought, behaved and related to people. Because we aren't perfect people, change is an ongoing process. It has to be worked at with the help of the Holy Spirit.

However, there are a number of ways *you* can block change.

So let's examine this flimsy excuse many use to leave a marriage. *If you "can't" change, it's because you don't want to change.* You've erected barriers to change. It's easier to be prideful, bitter, fearful or critical, to live in denial or to blame the other person. It's harder to work on yourself. So, let's talk.

Nothing Will Change If You Are Unwilling

An unwillingness to change is rooted in rebellion. It's that simple. Webster defines *rebellion* as "resistance or defiance to authority." Basically it's doing things your way vs. God's way. Remember the children of Israel? Rebellion was their main problem. Every time they got in trouble (which was often), it was because they did things their way. They went ahead of God's plan, devised their own and basically thought they knew better. They complained, criticized and worshiped idols. At the first sign of a crisis, they thought God abandoned them and they panicked. Thousands of years later, we're not that different.

There is an old saying, "It takes two to make a marriage and one to make a divorce." When divorce happens, it is often because one or both persons say, "I can't change." This unwillingness to do what it takes to make things right is witnessed time and again in clinical practice. If I had a dollar for every time people told me that they couldn't change, I'd be a rich woman.

A good marital therapist will eventually confront people on their refusal to change. This confrontation can evoke a nervous reaction. Hands wring. Eye contact is lost. Heads droop. People mumble under their breath, "This is who I am. I can't change." They mumble because they know they shouldn't be saying this. What they really mean is, "I don't *want* to change." I'd drop my head, too!

When I hear this, I usually sit silently. To say you can't

change underlies marital difficulty. A choice has been made. Change can't happen when you won't embrace it.

Update Your Virus Protection

Dale and Jennifer were nice young adults raised in decent families. Upon high school graduation, both attended the same Christian college. They dated, fell in love and married. For years they appeared to be a happy couple. But behind the scenes, tension mounted in the relationship.

The couple shared similar values, and they rarely if ever fought over the big issues of life. Jennifer was a fun-loving woman, but full of fear and anxiety. Although talented, she severely underrated her abilities. Her insecurity bothered Dale, but he never brought it up.

Dale was outgoing and well liked. He loved to socialize and tease people. His social confidence was strong, but he felt less than masculine due to his thin physical build and love of the arts. He hid this insecurity from his wife.

Dale and Jennifer focused on building their separate careers. Church attendance was erratic, and they stopped praying and reading their Bible together. Jennifer slipped in a quiet time here and there, but Dale was too busy.

As time passed, Dale and Jennifer's insecurities began to infect their marriage. Insecurities run like viruses on computers. Left unchecked, these viruses begin to corrupt the relationship.

Relationship virus protection involves two things that Dale and Jennifer ignored. First, they did not scan the feelings and thoughts of each other. *How are we doing? Are there any problems we haven't addressed? Do we need more time together? Are we sexually satisfied?* Both were too distracted to talk about their relationship.

The second needed scan was a spiritual one. *How tuned in to God are we? Do we have time for prayer, Bible reading and quiet moments to listen to and be with God?* With their spiritual guards down, insecurities took hold. How? Insecurity stems from a failed understanding of identity in Christ. The less time spent developing the spiritual self, the easier it was to be influenced by other things and people. Unprotected, they were open to all kinds of infections (like insecurity) that began to kill their relationship.

Lacking their daily dose of prayer and Bible reading, Dale and Jennifer began drifting apart. Their individual Christian walks suffered. They allowed unhealthy influences to infiltrate their thoughts and actions.

Jennifer looked to Dale to build her confidence. She was disappointed and felt overly dependent on him. Dale looked outside the marriage for affirmation regarding his masculinity. Secretly, Dale started accessing Internet pornography and flirting with women at his office. The women responded and reinforced his wish to be a desirable masculine figure. Other women built up his ego and made him feel sexually attractive. Dale found a way to build his self-esteem, but it was his way—not God's way.

When Dale and Jennifer finally sought marital counseling, Dale was close to having an extramarital affair. Clearly, the influences of pornography and flirtation were impacting his marriage. Jennifer tried to define herself through her husband and job. As both became problematic, she developed symptoms of anxiety and depression.

When I asked Jennifer if she was willing to change, to be less dependent on Dale for her identity, she responded, "Yes, of course. I don't know how, but I'll try. I don't want to find security in Dale or my work. I know that's not healthy. I thought my job might give me a better sense of who I am, but it hasn't. I feel pretty lost."

I turned to Dale. "You are flirting with trouble. Are you willing to stop the pornography you've allowed into your home and into your life?"

Dale answered, "Right now I'm comfortable with who I

am. I'm not doing anything I should be ashamed of. A few pictures and laughs with the women in my office are hardly crimes. Jennifer reacts because of her ever-growing insecurity. So the answer is no. I'm not willing because I don't think what I am doing is a big deal. You make it sound like I'm visiting prostitutes or something."

I made one last effort. "Dale, you know you are playing with fire. You are looking outside the marriage to meet intimacy needs. And you are engaging in things not pleasing to God, things that will bring negative consequences to your relationship."

Dale would not be moved. "I think I know best what I can handle. You and my wife are overreacting. I'm not willing to talk about this anymore."

It was clear. Dale was not interested in change. He knew it was wrong to expose himself to pornography and flirt with other women. He falsely believed he could handle the temptation. Besides, it felt good and built up his ego. It made him feel masculine and desirable.

Dale is no different from a lot of us who know we are wandering into troubled waters yet don't stop. Dale could have dealt with his problems, but he chose not to. Willfully flirting with danger and acting unwisely eventually brings destruction to a relationship. The end result can be divorce.

Whether it's sexual temptation or any other problem in your life, the defining moment is when you choose not to do anything about it. Basically, you embrace the lie, "I can't change. I won't change, I don't want to change, I don't need to change." Behind that lie is rebellion—a refusal to yield to divine control or submit your life to God's directives. Your stubborn resistance blocks full surrender to God—opening the door to trouble. The virus is in, and the infection process begins.

The Devil Didn't Make You Do It, but Temptation Is Real!

One reason we resist change is because we are deceived into thinking we don't need to change our sin nature. We minimize the fact that we have a formidable enemy whose entire purpose is to deceive and then to destroy. If he can entice you to give in to temptation, to sin or neglect your relationship with God, he has found a foothold. James 1:14–15 says that giving in to our desires gives birth to sin. Satan's purpose is to revive the sin nature in us as often as possible. He knows sin damages us and damages our relationships. He is acutely aware of our unhealthy desires, and he tries to pervert them.

Let's revisit the story of Eve for a moment to see how this works. Eve had a conversation with Satan. That was her first mistake. She should have told him to go take a crawl. Don't entertain your enemy/temptation for even a little while.

Satan, true to form, lied–"You will not die if you eat from the tree of the knowledge of good and evil. No, your eyes will be opened, and you will be like God." So Eve looked at the tree, saw it was good for food and pleasant to the eyes, and she ate. Then she gave some to Adam, who was with her, and he ate also. Adam rebelled against God's directive. Eve believed a lie.

As they ate, their eyes were opened. Instead of being like God, they realized they were naked. Oops, big mistake. Eve and Adam were in a world of hurt. Naked, they hid. When God called to Adam and asked him if he ate from the tree, Adam recalled the incident. "Eve gave it to me, and I ate." Eve, in turn, tells God, "I was deceived by the serpent."

Eve chose to believe a lie. She put her will above God's. Paul tells us that Eve was deceived, but Adam ate with full knowledge of wrongdoing (2 Cor. 11:3; 1 Tim. 2:14). Then, guilty and ashamed, they hid. Cursed they left the garden. Their disobedience perverted God's perfect plan.

Power Outage

Satan's game plan is to get you to pervert the will of God in your marriage by doing things your way. Obviously you can be deceived and sin like Eve, or you can choose to rebel against God's commands like Adam. Either way this opens the door to all kinds of insecurities and problems, like questioning your relationship and eventually embracing divorce.

Change Stoppers

Willingness to change is often preempted by something I call *change stoppers*. These are attitudes and actions that block change. Review this checklist to see if any of these prevent you from making necessary changes in your relationship.

Change stoppers

1 *Denial of a problem.* In Dale and Jennifer's case, Dale refused to admit he had a problem with pornography and masculine insecurity. You can't change problems you won't own.

2 *Self-centeredness.* Change doesn't fit your agenda, and it certainly doesn't work in your favor. You do only what's good for you, never considering the impact your choices have on others. Dale had a need and wanted it met regardless of the consequences.

3 *Pride and stubbornness.* You couldn't possibly be at fault. You rarely give in or admit wrong. Oh, you know there is a problem, but you refuse to deal with it due to pride or stubbornness.

4 *Fear of rejection.* You worry that if you make changes, your spouse won't love or accept you.

5 *Lack of trust.* Whether it's distrust of God or another person, it doesn't feel safe to make changes. You fear change may disrupt your relationship in a bad way, a way you can't handle.

6 *Unforgiveness.* You refuse to forgive your spouse for specific hurts and behaviors. Holding on to unforgiveness eventually leads to bitterness and blocks your ability to grow. It wreaks havoc on your physical and emotional self. It's also not scriptural.

7 *Anger.* You may refuse to change because you are angry—angry with God, a circumstance or somebody. Anger that stews over time or isn't addressed in relationships becomes destructive.

8 *You want everyone to be like you.* Individual differences are not tolerated. It's your way or no way. You don't need to change—the other person does.

9 *Prejudice.* It comes in all forms. You think you are somehow better than someone else. This sense of entitlement blocks empathy and leads to judgment.

10 *Insecurity.* Change equals uncertainty and raises your anxiety. You aren't sure of your decisions and actions. Therefore, you become ambivalent, making change more difficult.

11 *Money, power, status and prestige.* Why change when you have these things? You think they validate your current condition.

12 *Judgment and criticism.* These attitudes allow you to focus on the flaws of others—and not your own.

13 *Emotional shutdown.* This makes marital work very difficult, as you learned in previous chapters.

14 *Deliberate rejection of God's will.* When you know what you need to do and refuse to do it, you are settting yourself up for trouble.

15 *Too comfortable and satisfied.* Change is harder when we are comfortable or satisfied with the status quo. Comfort zones are inviting, even when they are dysfunctional.

16 *Lack of knowledge.* The Bible says we perish for lack of knowledge. Sometimes we don't change because we aren't familiar with the Word of God. Other times, we don't know how to problem-solve change.

17 *A sorry but unrepentant heart.* Sorry is a confession of the mouth. Repentance is a turning of heart direction. Repentance means you take action to change things or yourself. You move beyond confession to action.

18 *Wish to stay in the adolescent stage of life.* You may not want to grow up and accept responsibility. Why delay gratification? You are still living and thinking like an adolescent. Many addictions begin this way.

19 *Refusal to submit to God.* You refuse to make Him Lord of all your life. You want to be in control, and you think you can manage your life by yourself.

20 *No resistance.* You are easily defeated, give in and allow negative influences in your life. You don't recognize your authority in Christ. Not only are you told to resist the devil, but you have also been given complete authority over him in Christ. You don't exercise that authority.

21 *Lack of worship, prayer and meditation on God's Word.* You can't live a transformed life without an intimate relationship with Christ. Prayer, worship and meditation are vital to your growth.

22 *Lack of commitment to change.* You may have good intentions, but when the going gets rough, you revert to old habits.

23 *Stress.* Stress can wear you down if you don't manage it well. As a result, change is a low priority when you're all about surviving life's more pressing problems.

24 *Idol worship.* You put other things before God. I'm not talking little statues here. I'm talking about worshiping money, status, leisure, entertainment, sex, work–anything that you love more than God or that replaces Him in your life.

Move Over, Frank Sinatra; I Did It My Way, Too

Brian and Ellen needed help. They were in deep financial trouble (stress), which was affecting their marriage. Brian's series of bad investments had resulted in tremendous losses. Highly anxious over their financial future, he spent hours trying to problem-solve a way out of the mess he had created. He couldn't believe he was in this position. Having been a college business major, he knew better.

Ellen's father was a wealthy financial investor who could have helped. But Brian was uncomfortable asking for help from his father-in-law. The embarrassment was bad enough, but to be bailed out by good old dad was too much.

Brian and Ellen rarely talked about financial decisions. Brian admitted he didn't consult his wife and had never considered praying about investments. No one he knew ever did such a thing. Then he admitted borrowing tithe money to play the stock market when he was short on funds but sure the investments would pay off big.

The couple's financial problems were significant but workable. The bigger problem was Brian's lone-gun approach.

Neither God nor his wife was consulted. Brian confessed he had wanted to avoid any opposition to his plans. He wasn't a bad guy, just doing what many of us do—living life our way.

Self-reliance is held in high esteem in our culture. While God wants you to use the brainpower He gave you, He also wants to be an integral part of your life. He wants you to submit your will to His. That submission requires doing things the way God outlined in His Word. He promises to lead and direct—if you let Him. But you have to let Him.

Most of us go our own way like Brian. We end up in a mess and then wonder how we got there. We presume God isn't interested in our life or that He doesn't answer prayer, but in reality, we have left God out of the equation. Then when we do pray and immediate change doesn't happen, we blame Him and feel rejected.

Even though God is our ultimate resource, we rarely call on Him or hold Him to His Word. We think we can manage on our own. This was the original deception—"I can be like God. My way will work or perhaps be better than God's." This is a presumptuous lie. God has the big picture—not you.

There's a Power Outage

Why do so many people fail to change when it is so needed? One answer has to do with the above—they prefer *their way to God's way.* Yet others say they want to be obedient to God, but fail miserably. And since we have a plethora of resources, therapists, workshops and more to help people change, you would think more of us would live transformed lives. So why don't we? Look around. There's a power outage.

Over and over we are told we can overcome problems through our relationship with Christ. Yet, many of us struggle through our relationships and don't feel very powerful. Our problems overwhelm us. We forget the heritage we have been given in Christ. Consequently we don't use what's available for change. Instead we rely on ourselves. Sometimes this works, but more often it doesn't.

Oh, we've prayed the sinner's prayer. We've tried to be "good," and we even go to church, but we haven't plugged into His power. His Spirit doesn't electrify us. Instead, we illumine a spark here and there, then burn out. There is no power in our daily lives. We aren't that different from others around us who struggle with marital problems.

The reason for this is that we've plugged into the wrong power sources—ones that promise immediate energy but eventually fizzle out. Like the MTV bands, we are electrified for the moment, but there is no real power. Behind the hype, we find ourselves listless and unsure of who we are or where we are going.

Our uncertainty about God shows up in role confusion, distrust, acting out and sometimes more serious ways like eating disorders, depression, anxiety, poor self-image, anger, drinking, experimentation with drugs and partying. We try to plug in somewhere, anywhere, so we can feel alive and energized.

We search for the next thrill or challenge. We try a host of things—things that appeal to our flesh and our sense of self-reliance. We allow ourselves to be seduced. We bite the fruit! It looks so good.

These temporary power sources eventually burn out. When you plug into them, you will eventually be in the dark.

Temporary power sources

1. *The power of me.* What I make happen counts. I am basically good, able to make things happen because of my intellect, skills and abilities. I have within me what it takes to makes things happen. It's all up to me. Success defines me. I don't need God, because I am my own god.

2. *The power of materialism.* The more I get and own,

the happier I'll be. Power is in things, status and money. I get my identity through what I have—fashion, cars, big houses and expensive vacations.

3 *The power of relativism.* My journey is all that matters. Whatever is my experience is true and real for me. There are no absolutes, no rights and wrongs, only what I define to be truth. Power comes from experience, not biblical truth.

4 *The power of sexuality.* The more beautiful and perfect body I have, the more sensual I become, the more power I have to attract others and get what I need. I can use sex to persuade, to be close to others, to be loved. Sexual expression is used to gain power.

5 *The power of pop culture.* In the absence of strong family training, or simply by repeated exposure to pop culture, I have allowed pop culture to be my teacher. I have assimilated values and morals slowly through exposure to no moral standard. I justify my behavior and attitudes because I compare myself to the likes of Hollywood and sports stars. Who I am is constantly being seduced by plugging in to media that promotes hedonism and opposes biblical values.

These are only a few of many available power sources. All take us away from our need for God and connect us to power that won't accomplish much. The enemy loves this distraction. He tried it with Jesus. (See Matthew 4.) Remember how he took Jesus up to the mountain, showed Him all the kingdoms of the world and their glory and said, "Man, this is Yours if You will just bow down and worship me." The temptation was power.

The enemy will do anything to keep us away from the effective power source—Jesus Christ. He knows that when we disconnect from Him, we are ineffective in everything we do. We stay confused, purposeless and directionless.

If he can keep us distracted with power surges that eventually burn out, he's happy because he has accomplished his purpose. Our marriages fail, and we feel lost and confused about life. We have an idea about how life should be, but our experience doesn't match those expectations. We allow woundings from situations or people in our past to defeat us. Maybe we've lost our innocence, our virginity or even a hopeful view of the possibilities of our lives. We are lifeless, powerless and defeated. Change seems elusive.

If you feel powerless to make changes, it's time to get connected to the one interactive true God. There is no shortage of His power, but you must get connected. Plug in, dial up, log on. Incredible change is possible through the Holy Spirit working in concert with your efforts. He can illuminate areas for change and help you accomplish them.

Do what you are capable of doing, and then let the Holy Spirit do the rest. You are responsible to work on issues and relationship problems and to make good choices. But you need the power of the Holy Spirit to bring you lasting success. With God, your life can be transformed into something wonderful. But you have to desire it, be obedient and use the power.

Truth #7

I can change, but it requires desire, obedience and power.

To divorce-proof your marriage, you must be willing to change and let God direct your life. He is the reason change is even possible. On your own, change is a difficult process. With God's help, you can do it. Get rid of the change stoppers and conform your life to Christ's. Conforming is hard work and something most of us rebel against. But here are the steps.

Admit the Problem(s)

If you are going to change, you must first admit there is a problem. Whatever your reason for denial, lose it and start the work of improvement. Look, all of us have areas of needed improvement. We are all works in progress. Problems arise when we forget this.

Identify areas of needed change, and do something about them. Counseling helps people make changes. Get a competent, godly therapist, and get started. Or get in a small group and be accountable to others. Start listening to the feedback of friends and your spouse. Ask God to reveal areas of your life that need change. Refusal to do so is a set-up for divorce.

Change Your Heart

Pray for God to change your heart. You need to be softened to the things of God. The way to do this is to get into the Word, pray and worship God. I know this sounds like a simple idea. It is. Application is far tougher.

Couples ready to divorce have faltered somewhere in their relationships with God. In twenty years, I have never seen two people on fire for God, hungry for the things of the Spirit and moving in His will who are ready to divorce. For one thing, God doesn't direct you to do something against His own Word. Divorce is never commanded or encouraged in the Bible. So He is not going to direct you to do something He hates.

Couples have used this line on me before: "I've prayed about it, and God wants me to divorce. He sees how unhappy I am, and He wants me happy." How ridiculous! Don't try to manipulate God. God does not direct you to divorce. He *permits* divorce in cases of unrepentant hard hearts. He does *not* direct people to break covenant because of refusal to changes or reconciliation.

People who want out and use this excuse are really saying, "I'm going to do what I want to do, and no one is going to tell me otherwise." But people aren't this honest. Instead, they try to spiritualize a reason for divorce and hide behind a religious facade.

A change of heart is needed. Stop lying about what God wants you to do. Ask God to change your heart. Don't ask Him to make you happy. Ask Him to "Roto Rooter" your life and dig out all the blockages to change. This process won't always feel good. You will be emotionally drained, and you will come face to face with your own issues. But do face them. Don't run away.

Maybe you've been hurt by a spouse who keeps saying he or she will change—and doesn't. It's not your job to judge his or her heart. Maybe he or she is giving you a line, maybe not. Your job is to be willing to try. You will quickly see if the effort is real.

I'm often asked, "How many chances do you give a person to make necessary changes?" Decide the answer based on your covenant vows. God gives you unlimited grace and favor even when you don't deserve it.

Again, I am not talking about cases of violence and abuse. If there is potential physical harm, safety is your first concern. In those cases, work with a therapist who understands domestic violence, addiction or severe personality disturbances. I am talking directly to those who don't want to make needed changes and prefer to leave the marriage, thinking the grass is greener somewhere else. Stop wandering; graze in your covenant pasture. You have a lot of work to do.

Power Outage

Know God's Word

It sounds like a no-brainer to tell people to know the Word of God. But far too many Christians have never read much of the Bible. Bible reading is a discipline. It takes time to read it–and to study it. Bible reading is like a graduate course that never ends. You never really master all the information. Even when a passage seems to be familiar, the Holy Spirit can bring new revelation. Bible reading is not about nice stories. It's about continuously bathing in God's Word so you don't become spiritually dehydrated.

When you read the Bible, God speaks. You get to know Him, and you learn what He thinks, says and does. Think of it like this: When you dated your spouse, you wanted to know everything about that person–what he or she thought, ate, read, played. The more you knew, the easier it was to decide this was someone you wanted to trust, to be with.

The same is true of God. The more you know Him, the more you trust Him and want to learn more about Him. Reading His Word and spending time with Him in prayer are ways to become intimate with Him.

Most of us pretend we know Him when we don't. For many, God is an acquaintance–not an intimate friend. Quoting a few scriptures is not a personal relationship. Many people fail to live in dynamic power, so when difficulty comes, they panic, get depressed and fall apart.

Dig into the Word of God. Learn what your actions and attitudes are supposed to be. What guidelines are given for behavior and thoughts? What does godly character look like? For example, Galatians 5:22–23 lists the fruit of the Spirit–love, joy, peace, longsuffering, kindness, goodness, faithfulness, gentleness and self-control. Are these your character traits? Ungodly behavior is described as adultery, fornication, uncleanness, lewdness, idolatry, sorcery, hatred, contention, jealousy, outbursts of wrath, selfish ambition, dissensions, heresies, envy, murder, drunkenness and revelry (Gal. 5:19–21). If this list is more descriptive of your behavior and actions, you need change.

Many verses in the Bible provide explicit descriptions of the thoughts and behaviors that should be evident in the life of a Christian. In addition, numerous Bible studies are available on the subject of Christian living. With so much material at our disposal, we have no good reason to be illiterate and unplugged.

Submit to God

I have to admit it; a part of me doesn't like the word *submit*. It goes against my nature—as it probably does yours. *To submit* means to yield in surrender or compliance and obedience. When I married twenty-six years ago, I took the word *submit* out of my vows. I thought, *Why would I submit to some guy when I am probably as smart as he is? Maybe he should submit to me.*

Despite my egotism and complete misunderstanding of the biblical idea of submission, God blessed my marriage! I learned that it isn't difficult to submit to someone who is first submitted to God. That's the key—two people must be submitted to God.

Most marital problems stem from a lack of godly submission. If we believe that God's ways are best and what He has for us is good and perfect, we won't fight submission. If we, as spouses, are truly submitted in all things to God, then mutual submission to one another is not a negative experience that only feminists can save us from.

When one person in a marriage doesn't submit to God, problems result. Being unsubmissive to God is *spiritual rebellion,* and it has consequences. The Bible is full of stories of people who didn't choose God's way. They do not have happy endings. If you embrace Christianity, submission is part of the deal. But it's not the bad thing I was led to believe by the culture around me. When I submit to a loving God who deeply cares for me, it takes the pressure off. I don't have to have all the answers. And I have someone who is in control of my life who wants only my best.

Biblical submission has become politicized. It has nothing to do with politics, women's rights or the dominance of men. Submission is about letting God run your life despite your gender.

Submit your *entire* life to God, not just bits and pieces. Surrender your will completely. Most of us give a little here and there, but hold onto specific areas. Surrender all in order to divorce-proof your marriage. Giving yourself to God is an act of love on your part. He won't mistreat you.

Some of you have trusted people who have let you down or even hurt you. Consequently, you don't trust God, and you feel a need to control your life. But God hasn't let you down. Think about it. People mess up, but He doesn't leave or forsake you. His love is unconditional. His presence is always with you.

Maybe you feel alone or betrayed. You don't understand why certain things happened. It appears God is not on the scene. But He is. Just because you don't understand the circumstances or can't control someone's behavior doesn't mean God abandoned you. Don't go by your feelings or by the way things look for the moment. Trust God to be true to His Word. He will. Take a leap of faith and make a full surrender.

Practice What You Have Learned

After you have asked God to change your heart, have learned to know Him intimately through His Word and have submitted to His will, you must begin to practice what you have learned. This is where the rubber meets the road. It's one thing to know what you are supposed to do, and another thing to do it!

Remember that you have change-producing help—prayer and the Holy Spirit. Spiritual change brings behavioral change. First, determine that your behavior and thought life will line up with God's Word. Then pray and ask the Holy Spirit to help you make it happen. He will give you the power to accomplish your goals.

Ben had to do this. Ben had a terrible anger problem. His rage stemmed from living with an abusive father who criticized and belittled him as a child. Ben hated the way his anger unleashed on his wife, Beth. He sought therapy to help him identify the hot buttons for his anger and to teach him anger control strategies.

Ben also asked God to help him. He studied scriptures on anger and self-control. He knew how he was supposed to behave with his wife. Ben worked in therapy to learn anger cues and strategies for self-control. When his anger was aroused, he practiced those control strategies and prayed. As he worked to calm himself down, he asked the Holy Spirit to give him the self-control he needed for the moment. He knew that without the help of the Spirit, lasting change was a question mark.

You can access the same power Ben did to overcome patterns of behavior that you want to change. It may take work, but it can be done. If you have lived years behaving one way, change may not be instant. Unhealthy patterns of behavior are learned and must be unlearned. But with the power of the Holy Spirit, the change process doesn't have to take a lifetime.

Don't get discouraged when you slip into an old behavior pattern. Learn to recognize the old pattern, then change it. If your spouse is trying to change, don't pounce when he or she makes a mistake. Instead, point out the problem but remind your spouse of the new way to handle the situation.

Reinforce steps toward change. Change is a process that God sometimes miraculously abbreviates.

Reinforce Those Changes

Change is not easy for most of us. When you make a change in the right direction, reinforce it. Behavior changes with positive reinforcement. Sometimes that reinforcement must come from within. Let's return to Ben and Beth.

Ben was determined to get his anger under control, but he was married eight years before he had a change of heart. Beth feared Ben's anger. He never hit her, but he came close. He was physically intimidating, so Beth's fear was grounded in reality.

As Ben began making changes and exercising self-control, Beth sat silent. In therapy, she was glad Ben was changing but didn't trust the change to last. I encouraged her to share this with him. Ben was upset that his wife wasn't more positive. Change wasn't easy.

What Ben failed to recognize was the full impact his threatening behavior had on the relationship. A few weeks of appropriate anger control did not wipe out eight years of history. Beth had reason to be hesitant. She needed to see *sustained* change. Ben needed to recognize how his behavior contributed to Beth's uncertainty. But at the moment, he was angry at Beth's unenthusiastic response and was ready to give up. Why should he try if his wife didn't recognize his efforts?

I gave him three reasons for continuing his quest to change:

1 Even if Beth never said a word to him, his behavior was still wrong.

2 Beth's behavior did not determine his.

3 He didn't fully understand how his past influenced the present.

"Stop looking to Beth," I counseled, "for strokes to do what you should have learned to do years ago—control your temper." Yes, it would be great if she would pat him on the back, but under the circumstances he should understand her hesitancy. He needed to reinforce his own behavior. He was doing the right thing. Anger control was the sign of a healthy man. He should pat himself on the back for making this change. But to expect Beth to be his biggest fan at the first sign of change was asking too much. She had been traumatized by his past behavior and was just now allowing herself to lower a little of her guard. Over time, as Ben demonstrated consistent change, she would relax and have positive words for him. Patience was needed here.

In the next session, Beth told Ben that she was very happy he was controlling his anger. But she also voiced her fears that he might resort to past behavior. Ben apologized for not understanding how his anger had created fear for Beth. He now realized how his behavior hurt his wife. Ben took responsibility for his actions that had created the relationship problem. Before Beth would feel the freedom to respond positively, he had to prove himself trustworthy.

The real question was, "What was motivating Ben's change?" Was it guilt, Beth's fear, the therapist, the threat of divorce, or were other factors motivating him? Hopefully he was motivated by his sin. He needed to recognize that his behavior was so un-Christlike it had harmed his relationship.

Change is usually progressive. If you can encourage your spouse along the way, do so—it helps tremendously. Patience is greatly needed on the part of both spouses. And patience is not a valued virtue in our society. Our disposable culture says that if something doesn't measure up immediately, discard it and move on to the next thing. This mentality has taken hold in marriage as well. If your partner has problems, divorce him or her. There is someone else out there who is nicer, kinder, richer, sexier or whatever.

Don't fall prey to the "if it's broken, get rid of it" mentality. If you need to change, get help, identify the problem, correct it and live a transformed life. People often choose therapy because it is one place where someone will work patiently with them on change. The growing popularity of therapy relates, in part, to the unwillingness of others to hold people accountable for change. Therapists hold people accountable and reinforce steady progress.

Having said that, you don't necessarily need a therapist to change behavior. You can begin now. If your spouse has received the brunt of your problematic behavior, don't look to that person to cheer your changes immediately. Look for encouragement from people who have not had to live with your problematic behavior. If your change is genuine and lasting, your spouse will eventually become your number-one fan.

All of us like to be praised. It helps us change. Our goal is to be more like Christ. But your partner may not be your first cheerleader. If he or she does not cheer your efforts, don't throw in the towel and quit. Your desire to change should come from within—by the prompting of the Spirit—if you are plugged in to God's power.

Embracing change isn't easy, but it is necessary in order to divorce-proof your marriage. Marriages fail because people refuse to model Christ in thought and behavior. Rebellion takes many different forms, one of which is the refusal to line up your behavior and thoughts with God's. Someone else may accept you just the way you are, but you still won't please God if your behavior is problematic.

No more excuses. You can change. You have access to powerful change agents—therapists, godly men and women, books, seminars, workshops and teaching. But the most powerful change agent is the Holy Spirit. Access what God has given you. Say no to the lie "I can't change" and yes to transformation. Change is possible with desire, obedience and the power of the Holy Spirit.

Review

Lie #7   *I can't change—this is who I am; take it or leave it.*

Truth #7   *I can change, but it requires desire, obedience and power.*

Divorce-Proofing Strategies

- Dedicate your life to ongoing change. No one has arrived yet!

- Run relationship and spiritual virus scans.

- Do not be deceived or willfully choose rebellion.

- Identify and rid yourself of change stoppers.

- Unplug from ineffective power sources. Plug in to the interactive God.

- Admit you have a problem.

- Ask God to change your heart.

- Know God's Word so you can evaluate your behavior against a standard.

- Submit to God. Be obedient to His directives.

- Practice what you've learned.

⟳ Reinforce those changes, and stay accountable for your behavior.

⟳ Access the transforming power of the Holy Spirit to make those changes last.

CHAPTER 10

Infidelity

Lie #8

There has been an affair.
We need to divorce.

I did not have sex with that woman." Can we ever forget that fiery denial from former President Bill Clinton concerning his now infamous relationship with White House intern Monica Lewinsky? Thanks to detailed media reports of intimate conversations and sexual behavior, the whole nation was discussing what *does* and *does not* constitute marital infidelity.

So what is *infidelity*? Is it an act of the heart, a break of trust, a physical breach of the martial vows? Can you be emotionally involved outside your marital covenant and still be faithful? If you are physical, but stop short of intercourse, are you OK? How far is too far?

"Too Far" Is When You Can't Tell Your Spouse!

Tom was a bright guy who found himself restless and bored at his office. He began flirting with a coworker. The two started having lunch together and met occasionally after work for a drink. Eventually they became physically involved, but they never had sexual intercourse. Fearing he might step over his self-imposed line, Tom came to therapy. His first question was, "Have I really been unfaithful to my wife? I haven't had intercourse, and we haven't been fully undressed together. We've done a lot of kissing and fondling, but does that really count?"

I asked Tom, "If you told your wife what you just told me, what would she say?" Silence. Tom knew the answer.

Infidelity Is More Than Sex

Infidelity is a breach of trust, a breaking of the covenant, a betrayal of the relationship. It goes beyond sexual intercourse to include the physical, emotional and thought life of a person.

God wants you to be faithful to your spouse. Jesus takes a hard line on extramarital relationships, addressing both the heart and impure thoughts (Matt. 5:27–28; 19:18–19). According to His words, emotional adultery is as serious as sexual immorality. I know this sounds incredible in our society. I have heard people laugh at the very notion. Why? Because lust, the root of infidelity, is encouraged in our secularized culture. Sex is pleasurable. Sex sells. Self-restraint is not the American way.

But infidelity requires meeting a need outside the boundary of your covenant. You find someone who attracts you for one reason or another, and you experience desire for that person. A conscious choice is made to entertain that desire and toy with it. When desire is entertained, the outcome is usually gratification. Once we choose to gratify ourselves, the line is crossed.

Infidelity is almost always draped in secrecy and lies. The marital vow is breached, and the cover-up begins. Obviously this breeds guilt, and that's appropriate. But then guilt must be pushed out of the mind in order to continue the infidelity. A vicious cycle ensues—extramarital involvement, lying, cover-up, guilt, pushing the guilt away, more extramarital behavior and so on.

While *adultery* is a term used to describe sex outside of marriage, *infidelity* is about sexual dishonesty. If you hide any acts, thoughts or inappropriate emotional attachments from your partner, it may be because you have gone too far.

Chronic Stress Coupled With Emotional Distance

Quiet, attractive Angela met Sam at college and agreed to marry him after graduation. Unexpectedly she became pregnant. After long and arduous discussions about what to do with her career when the baby arrived, the couple decided Angela would stay home and raise the baby.

When their daughter, Alex, was three years old, Angela began noticing Sam's absence at dinner. Sam found every excuse possible to resume his pre-baby life. He joined the health spa, played basketball with the guys and hung out at bookstores until late hours.

Sam talked more and more about his life away from Angela. He loved his daughter, Alex, but part of him resented her premature entry into his marital life. Conversations with his once interesting wife now focused on potty training and mundane home matters. The mutual interest he and Angela shared in politics was put on the back burner. Angela, who once was up on current affairs and political issues, barely had time to shower. Sam longed for their former companionship, and he started to resent the demands motherhood made on Angela. Bored and unwilling to confront the problem, he became active in a local political campaign. Slowly he turned his interests away from his wife and toward other things.

Angela was adjusting to motherhood, too. Her plans for a career in medical research were clearly on hold. With dreams delayed, she resigned herself to the reality of the baby. Although Alex was unplanned, someone had to be responsible. She and Sam grew more distant with every passing day. Angela never talked about the changes, but she resented Sam's freedom and his neglect. She kept those feelings inside, too exhausted to deal with her husband.

At the campaign office, Sam met a young single woman, Sheila, who loved to talk about the current political climate. Sheila's passion for politics was attractive, and a growing sexual tension between the two began to develop. They spent long hours together.

Angela worried. She sensed Sam's distancing more and more from her. Nights away from home became more frequent as campaign business consumed all his free time. Worried that she was going crazy and becoming a jealous wife, she called for an appointment.

"I suspect Sam is having an affair. Things have been tense between us for months. He's making excuses to stay at campaign headquarters. There are unaccountable expenses on the credit cards. He's sexually distant. And I know this sounds really crazy, but he smells different when he comes home.

"Sam tells me I'm paranoid and reading too much into his late nights. So I've tried to ignore the red flags. I tell myself to calm down and that my marriage is OK. Sam is just going through a rough time adjusting to parenthood. But it's been three years, and things haven't changed, so I decided to talk to someone about my suspicions."

What Angela discovered was that Sam and Sheila *were*

having an extramarital affair. Her suspicions were accurate. When she confronted Sam, he lied. When she hired a private investigator to find the truth, Sam finally admitted to his relationship with Shelia.

Sam and Angela sat uncomfortably on a therapy couch. Angela tearfully began. "I've been hurt beyond anything I've ever experienced, but I want to make things right. We have a baby. We are young. Maybe we can work things out and put this behind us. I'd like to try."

Sam didn't react. He stared into space for a moment. Without ever making eye contact with Angela, he glanced at me. "I want a divorce. We've grown apart. She's not the woman I married. I know this hurts, but I think I've really found my soul mate. I can't go back to this baby thing or to Angela. And I really don't think I can give up Sheila right now. Look, this gives Angela biblical grounds for a divorce. I'm at fault."

"I don't want grounds," Angela responded. "I want my husband back. I want him to honor his covenant. I want a father who lives with his daughter. How can you just walk away?" Angela sat in stunned disbelief.

Sam moved his things out the next day.

Marital satisfaction drops significantly for many couples after the birth of the first baby. It can be an event that sends an already disconnected twosome down a troubled path. When a couple lacks friendship and intimacy prior to a birth, the new baby can further widen the gulf between them.

Other Reasons for Affairs

Therapists know that about half of all marital therapy involves an extramarital affair. However, a spouse may not know when an affair has taken place. Whether affairs are secretive or out in the open, they are damaging and create significant family crisis.

Divorce Proofing Your Marriage

The birth of a baby (or other life events) is only one of many reasons people have affairs. Affairs usually begin with friendship. Time together increases opportunity to build intimacy, so coworkers are often chosen. Couples who are emotionally distant and don't talk are vulnerable. Usually a hurting person meets another hurting person, and a need for intimacy is shared. Typically sex helps men feel virile and boosts their ego, while women look for someone to love and appreciate them. Younger couples are more at risk.

People who have affairs generally believe they are wrong. Obviously, believing an affair is morally wrong doesn't deter everyone. While survey data indicate that 15 percent of women and 25 percent of men *confess* to "straying," it's not the universal behavior our media and pop culture seem to portray.[1] Affairs are not normative behavior.

Affairs that are emotionally based or have limited sexual intimacies other than intercourse make up about 20 percent of all people who admit to infidelity. More men have affairs, but women are gaining ground.[2]

A double standard exists when it comes to affairs. Divorce is more likely when the woman has the affair. Unfaithful women are viewed more negatively than unfaithful men in many cultures—including ours.

Usually affairs are fueled by:

- Marital dissatisfaction

- Family problems

- Friendships that have become too close

- "Falling in love" with another person

- Physical separation

- Spiritual decline in one's intimate relationship with God

Infidelity

- ◯◯ Wish for sexual fulfillment
- ◯◯ Search for identity and self-esteem
- ◯◯ Convenience and sexual stimulation
- ◯◯ Liberal values
- ◯◯ Escape from reality
- ◯◯ Rebellion
- ◯◯ Satanic influence
- ◯◯ Wish for fun vs. the work of marriage
- ◯◯ Intimacy problems
- ◯◯ Need to feel loved or befriended

Those who resist affairs do so because of:

- ◯◯ Commitment to the marital covenant
- ◯◯ Strong trust established with partner
- ◯◯ Religious values
- ◯◯ Moral standards
- ◯◯ Evaluation of the negative consequences (potential harm to the marriage)
- ◯◯ The risk of STDs (amazingly, fear of contracting AIDS has not been identified as a deterrent)[3]
- ◯◯ A strong personal relationship with an intimate God
- ◯◯ Healthy sense of self-identity, maturity and self-esteem

Would it surprise you to learn that most unfaithful partners do not divorce in order to marry the person with whom he or she had an affair? Often the affair is a symptom of underlying marital unhappiness and propels the partner outside the relationship. Or the affair itself causes marital unhappiness.

It's also not true that affairs are about great sex. The other person is not necessarily better looking or better in the bedroom. Affairs are more about friendships and emotional attachment. Sex is usually not the primary purpose of an affair. Friendship and closeness are.

The loathed "other woman" did not entice your spouse to have an affair. Affairs are purposeful behavior. Rarely are people forced into an affair. So stop blaming the floozy for being the persuasive sexpot who lured him against his will. Or stop raging at the romantic guy who took advantage of your vulnerable wife. It takes two willing bodies to tango.

All in all, infidelity is destructive and causes great damage to marriages. However, an affair needn't be a death sentence. Divorce is not always inevitable in the face of an affair. That belief is a lie. Perhaps the bigger spiritual lie is that an affair *demands* divorce. After all, adultery is a biblical out. So why not take it? You've been wronged. Why stay with someone who betrays you? You deserve better. You're entitled to a divorce.

Truth #8

Affairs are serious and damaging, but not beyond repair and reconciliation.

Affairs are usually symptomatic of deeper marital problems—typically problems that existed before the affair. Obviously the affair adds even more. While I would never say that affairs help to strengthen a marriage, I will say that working through an affair can bring a couple to a new level of intimacy. Divorce is not the inevitable outcome.

Infidelity

Over my twenty years of practice, I have seen numerous couples put rocky marriages back together after the devastation of an affair. With God's help, forgiveness, repentance, an understanding of what caused the affair and a willingness to work on problems through marital therapy, marriages can come through the process of infidelity stronger and recommitted. The problem is many Christian couples are reluctant to work on forgiveness followed by reconciliation. They take their biblical "out" and run with it.

Remember, divorce is never commanded or even encouraged in the Bible. But forgiveness and reconciliation are. Some Christian couples I have treated do not appear any different from their secular counterparts when it comes to dealing with a damaged marriage. They use their legitimate justification to leave. Often they're willing to forgive, but reconciliation is another matter.

Because we experience forgiveness from a loving heavenly Father, we can forgive others, even for an affair. Forgiveness is a crucial step in the healing process, but more is needed. Beyond forgiveness is reconciliation.

Affairs Are Traumatic— the Admission

Rhonda had never seen a therapist before her husband announced he was having an affair with another woman. The shock of his disclosure was enormous. She repeatedly asked herself, *How could I have missed the signs and been so naive? Have I been in denial of our marital problems?*

Rhonda didn't consider herself prone to anxiety. However, since the disclosure she has had several anxiety attacks. She could be doing laundry and suddenly feel short of breath. Or she might be reading a book and feel her heart pounding and her palms sweating. Watching television could send her into an agitated state, especially if the program contained reference to an extramarital affair. Sleep eluded her. She had no appetite and was rapidly losing weight.

Even though her husband claimed to have stopped seeing the "other" woman, Rhonda felt uneasy and deeply betrayed. She found herself obsessively thinking about the other woman in intimate conversations with her husband. When she closed her eyes, she envisioned him holding that woman's hand and caressing her.

Rhonda found herself monitoring her husband's every movement. Little things upset her. She became highly suspicious. She couldn't shake the mental picture of her husband in bed with another woman. Intrusive thoughts flooded her mind. Rhonda felt as if she were losing it. She needed to bounce all this off of a therapist to see if she was going crazy.

When an affair has been found out, it is common to have reactions like Rhonda's. Anxiety attacks and grieflike symptoms are normal responses to the breach of marital covenant. In many ways, the reactions of the noninvolved spouse are similar to posttraumatic stress symptoms associated with emotional, physical and sexual abuse. The reality of an affair awakens a deep sense of loss. At times, you may feel you are going crazy. This is normal.

Couples who deal with an extramarital affair do have higher rates of depression than couples who come to marital therapy for other reasons.[4] Some spouses even become suicidal. It's also not uncommon to have homicidal rage toward the lover.

Given this emotional intensity and instability, the safety of people involved must always be considered. While not all people will act out their intense feelings of betrayal and rage, the risk is real. Turn on the nightly news, and you'll get a glimpse of what betrayed people can do!

It's important to know that you won't feel like this forever. In fact, what you feel is valid given the circumstances. The intensity is strongest when the affair is found out because of the reality of the deception and betrayal. The goal is to manage those intense feelings so you don't become incapacitated by them. Take these steps:

- Allow yourself to feel whatever comes.

- Don't deny the intensity of your emotions.

- Work with a therapist who can help you express what you feel and help you manage those feelings.

- Pour your heart out to God. He hears your pain, and He promises to comfort you even in difficult times.

For the one who has committed the betrayal, you can't avoid talking about what happened. You will want to avoid the subject and reel back at every mention of the affair and the pain you caused. That's part of the cross you bear initially—seeing how your choice impacts your partner.

Spiritual Consequences

Not only do you suffer emotionally from affairs, but spiritual intimacy is also blocked. Affairs are clearly sinful. Engaging in that behavior is willfully sinning against God's law. Until that sin is confessed and true repentance occurs, a person cannot be free to lead a vibrant Christian life. Often psychiatric symptoms result when you carry the guilt of unconfessed sin.

My experience has taught me that affairs must honestly be brought out into the open in order for a couple to have a chance to reconcile. One myth is that if you talk about the affair, the person will leave. In reality, not talking about it increases the probability of divorce.

When I hear someone say, "We grew apart. We just

couldn't communicate any more. We are different people," I wonder about an affair cover-up. In many cases, marriages end without the truth of infidelity ever surfacing. Hidden sin blocks healing. So the first step is to admit the sin.

After the Admission of an Affair

Dan was devastated. His wife, Susan, was supposed to be in Cleveland on business. Instead she was seen vacationing in the Virgin Islands with a male coworker. The betrayal took him by surprise. He couldn't believe Susan would risk their ten-year marriage for another man.

Dan called a therapist. Susan admitted to the affair. She apologized profusely and cut off all contact with the other man. The hurt and anger in Dan's face was hard to bear. Susan hoped that after she apologized and admitted her sin, Dan would get over the affair. She felt that by stopping the relationship, she had signaled to Dan that she wanted to reconcile.

But Dan couldn't stop thinking about the betrayal. He found himself obsessing about the other man. He worried that Susan would be unfaithful again. Then he felt guilty. Susan had apologized over and over, promising never to have an affair again. She went back to church, talked to the minister and placed herself under the accountability of a woman's group. But Dan's anxiety kept him from sleep.

Dan began to sense Susan was angry with him for not "getting over" the affair. Susan said, "Forget it ever happened. Why are you still talking about it when it's over?" She was frustrated by his nervous anxiety whenever the phone rang late at night, and she resented his constant questioning.

Dan and Susan represent many couples stuck in the aftermath of an affair. They think that just because the affair is acknowledged, things should go back to the way they were before. They don't recognize the traumatizing aftereffects that are part of the process. Nor have they dealt with marital issues that culminated in an affair.

Dan never truly acknowledged his feelings about the infidelity. He was too afraid Susan would leave the marriage. He felt vulnerable due to his financial dependence on her salary. Historically, he avoided marital conflict. He'd pretend to believe everything was great even when it wasn't.

Susan had apologized but showed little remorse. She had broken the marital covenant, and she expected Dan to be over it much too quickly. She failed to understand the trauma her husband experienced or that the apology just wasn't enough.

Susan needed to do . . .

- Share her feelings of remorse more than once.
- Allow Dan to question her.
- Give reassurances to Dan as needed.
- Be empathetic for the pain her actions caused Dan.
- Understand that Dan's reactions were typical.
- Learn to share her emotions—including her fear that Dan may leave.
- Be patient; her husband needed time.
- Identify what caused her to stray from her relationship and make changes.

Dan needed to . . .

- Have time to process, talk and explore his feelings more deeply.
- Be assured that his posttraumatic stresslike symptoms (difficulty sleeping and concentrating, hypervigilance and intolerance for things that brought up memories of the affair) were normal.

- ◯◯ Be allowed to question Susan whenever he needed reassurance.

- ◯◯ Not feel guilty when he needed to talk more about what happened.

- ◯◯ Start addressing his conflict avoidance and dependence issues.

Admission of infidelity is just the first step in a long process. The betrayal raises complicated emotions, which usually do not fade away without additional work. A one-time apology is never enough to cover the reactions of the partner. Your partner needs to forgive, but also to process his or her reactions over time. The one who committed the offense needs to be patient, remorseful and humble.

The person who had the affair needs to accept questions about what happened and tolerate the new hyper-vigilance for a while. It takes time to restore trust. The other spouse worries about recurrence and betrayal happening a second time. The betrayed one thinks, *If an affair happened once and I didn't know, couldn't I be missing it again? I'd better stay on guard. I must pay attention to any sign so I won't be made a fool again.*

Steps to Take After the Admission

Step 1: Stop the affair, and make a "no more contact" rule.

If your spouse cannot agree to this step, he or she hasn't completely ended the affair. Usually this means the spouse is ambivalent about reconciliation. He or she may be having doubts or be unwilling to give up the affair for the uncertainty of the marriage.

If the affairee tries to contact your spouse, follow this guideline—your spouse will share the information and what steps he or she took to end the contact. Contact must end or there is no proceeding.

Step 2: Acknowledge that the feelings related to the crisis are real and difficult.

Don't minimize feelings or try to squelch them. Anxiety, grief, depression and rage are common reactions, as we discussed, and need to be managed and tolerated for the time being.

Step 3: Tell the story.

As painful as this is, I usually advocate for the person who had the affair to tell what happened while allowing the spouse to ask questions. The timing and planning of this can be worked out with a therapist. The kind and depth of questions differs from person to person. Some people want to know every detail. Others don't want to know much because of the mental pictures painted. People vary in their need to know details and events. The guilty spouse needs to allow for questions and answer factually and truthfully.

There are therapists who will agree to keep an affair secret as long as it stops. In the Christian faith, the biblical directive is to confess sin one to another. The sin of infidelity is against your spouse. You have broken the covenant that involves you, your spouse and God. Thus, confession is necessary if healing is to occur.

I won't pretend this confession is easy to do. The obvious fear is that the spouse will leave or divorce because they have grounds. I've seen this happen. It's the risk you take because you can't live with hidden sin.

I've also watched Christian spouses use confession to win sympathy from friends and to move ahead with divorce even when their partner wants to reconcile. A Christian must not malign his or her partner to the Christian community and must make every effort to reconcile. If your spouse refuses reconciliation, there is not much that can be done. However, you need to be open to the idea.

Step 4: Begin to identify what made you vulnerable to an affair.

This does not mean you are excusing or justifying the affair. The person who acted out is responsible for his or her behavior. But it is important to figure out what may have led to this behavior so that those problems can be worked on, repaired and prevented.

The person who had the affair is still accountable and wrong. But knowing the cause helps the repair process and can prevent future problems. For example, was the affair spontaneous—a momentary giving into temptation helped along by alcohol or drugs? Was it permitted because of a need to experiment or a permissive attitude? Was it an unhealthy reaction to life stress—unresolved problems, lack of intimacy, developmental issues, unresolved childhood issues, expectations, power, entitlements, control or sexual dysfunction? Did it involve romantic love and emotional involvement or repetitive patterns of sexual addiction and pornography? Discovering the root problems helps you know what has to be corrected.

Step 5: What did the affair mean in the relationship?

For example, was the affair a way to avoid life responsibilities? Was it an act of entitlement for a lousy life? Was it something men just do and women need to accept? Was it a way to hurt your partner after being hurt? Was it a reaction to neglect of your relationship with God? Whatever the meaning of the affair, correct the problem or faulty view.

Step 6: Forgive.

As mentioned, people get confused on the difference between forgiveness and reconciliation. They are not the same. Forgiveness is something you do by yourself. Forgiveness does not always mean you will reconcile. It doesn't mean you are saying what the person did was not wrong. It means you are willing to let go of an offense no matter what happened. Biblically we are called to do this. It is vital to our Christian growth and spiritual condition. Unforgiveness leads to bitterness. Bitterness brings calamity to our body and soul.

You give forgiveness to others, not because they deserve it but because Christ forgave you. It is His way of doing things. Forgiveness releases the person from the offense and releases you from hanging on to the offense. Forgiveness isn't always instantaneous. Fallout from an affair heals with time and the rebuilding of trust.

When you forgive you let go of negative emotion (anger, resentment, hurt) and thoughts (judgment) toward the person who hurt you. Forgiveness is an unconditional gift to those who may not ask or deserve it.

Step 7: Release the person from judgment.

In the natural, this is hard to do. You want your spouse to pay for the pain he or she caused. Our culture is big on judgment, and the church is no exception. Your spouse will suffer consequences, but it is not your place to judge the person continuously and throw the affair in his or her face. God is the judge. Let Him do His job, and you do yours—work on forgiveness and moving past this traumatizing event.

Step 8: Rebuild romance and care.

Try to recall moments of attraction, caring and thoughtfulness. Rebuild the friendship that may have dropped off along the way. Determine to say positive and loving things to your partner—not out of guilt but because you must build respect and caring again. The stronger your friendship, the easier it will be to rebuild the relationship. You have to rediscover the man or woman who attracted you in the first place. Focus on the positives and build on them. This doesn't mean you ignore what has happened and stop talking about it. It simply means you have to renew romance in the relationship. Go out on dates, talk in front of the fire, spend time together doing something enjoyable and pay attention to the emotional life of your spouse. Again, this takes time and will feel uncomfortable at first.

Step 9: Move toward reconciliation.

Reconciliation is a process between two people that moves beyond forgiveness. One person can forgive, but it takes two to reconcile. You may have to lay down differences—agree to disagree on some points, accept a flawed individual and work hard to mend broken parts of the relationship—but it can be done.

Except for cases of ongoing harm or repeated, unrepentant infidelity and hardness of heart, reconciliation should be the goal—not divorce. Reconciliation requires a mutual restoring of trust between two people that comes about through trustworthy behaviors. Forgiveness is a part of reconciliation.

It's not enough to resolve differences or forgive. Jesus tells us to be reconciled one to another (Matt. 5:24), to restore our relationships with each other and to live in unity together when possible. He promises to restore the years the locust have eaten (Joel 2:25), which refers to God's grace after repentance. Trust God. When confession is honestly made and a turning of behavior gives proof of repentance, God can do miraculous things. But both partners have to be willing to reconcile.

We serve a God who is "able to do exceedingly abundantly above all that we ask or think" (Eph. 3:20). God is in the business of restoring what's broken and making it new. Don't give up on your relationship because of an affair. Don't buy the lie that tells you your marriage will end in divorce. Refuse that lie. Ask God to give you a brand-new love, stronger than before.

I heard a sermon over twenty years ago by psychologist Richard Dobbins, head of Emerge Ministries, that has impacted so many. He challenged people to pray for disturbing memories that often linger after we do something shameful. He was addressing people who had confessed sin and repented, but who were struggling to be released from guilt, intrusive thoughts and/or vivid memories.

We can repent over past mistakes but continue to be plagued by guilt that takes us nowhere but into self-condemnation. Dr. Dobbins prayed for memories to be healed and people to be set free from self-reproach. People poured down the aisle sobbing. Many were released from years of self-condemnation. It wasn't that sin was forgotten; it was that it no longer had the power to shame and produce inappropriate guilt.

It was during this evening I finally understood that when God covers a sin, He blots it out.

> **There is therefore now no condemnation to those who are in Christ Jesus, who do not walk according to the flesh, but according to the Spirit. For the law of the Spirit of life in Christ Jesus has made me free from the law of sin and death.**
>
> —Romans 8:1–2

What a gift!

It is possible for God to free us (once we've gone through the reconciliation process) from intrusive thoughts related to past affairs. In God, the *past* is not a prologue to the *future* because of the cross of Calvary and the resurrection of Jesus Christ. That is radical when you think about it. Not only can we be forgiven and reconciled—but we can be freed from persistent guilt and condemnation!

Consequently, if you have experienced an affair in your marriage, it's possible to survive it, repair the brokenness and be cleansed from the guilt. The truth is that all things broken can be repaired through our relationship with Christ first, then with our spouse. Don't believe the lie that a broken covenant is beyond repair.

Review

Lie #8 — *There has been an affair. We need to divorce.*

Truth #8 — *Affairs are serious and damaging, but not beyond repair and reconciliation.*

Divorce-Proofing Strategies

Ask yourself these questions if you are having an affair or are uncertain if you've crossed the line. Then take the steps outlined in this chapter to repair damage from an affair and bring reconciliation to the relationship.

- How would my spouse feel if he or she knew?

- Would my behavior or thoughts be a betrayal of the trust in my marriage?

- Are my behavior and thought life pleasing to God?

The person who had the affair needs to:

- Admit the affair.

- Stop all contact with the affairee.

- Tell the story and allow your partner to talk about it and ask questions.

Infidelity

- Be empathetic to the pain you have caused, but don't live in condemnation if you are truly repentant.

- Reestablish spiritual intimacy with God.

- Get to the root of your straying behavior in order to prevent a future betrayal.

- Be patient with your partner's emotional process.

- Ask God to give you a new love for your partner.

- Begin to rebuild love and friendship.

- Ask God to free you from lingering guilt and intrusive thoughts of the affair.

- Reconcile.

The person who has been betrayed needs to:

- Understand that feelings of trauma are normal and will not stay forever.

- Be free to acknowledge those feelings.

- Ask for reassurance whenever needed

- Ask questions when needed.

- Explore and resolve relationship issues that led to the affair or were caused by the affair.

- Forgive (it may be a process that takes time).

- Release the spouse from judgment.

- Be willing to reconcile unless there are safety issues or ongoing betrayal that needs to be addressed.

- Let go of self-condemnation.

- Rebuild lost love and trust.

Both must be willing to talk about the affair and want reconciliation. If you refuse reconciliation, you are out of alignment with God's way of thinking. You are responsible for wanting something God doesn't—a divorce.

CHAPTER 11

Cheap Grace

Lie #9

It doesn't matter what I do;
God will forgive me.

first grappled with the concept of grace when I was a teenager. Oh, don't get me wrong; grace was extended to me
plenty of times during childhood. But it wasn't until I hit
adolescence that I realized God's grace could be manipulated for personal benefit.

Temptation to sin seemed ever present during my teen
and young adult years. Being "good" wasn't easy. One day I
walked the straight and narrow path of Christian living. The
next day I was ready to party. Whatever the course of the
week, it seemed I (and the rest of my youth group) always
ended up at the same place on Sunday nights–the altar. God
and I had to do some serious talking.

After months of this Sunday night ritual, altar trips

became automatic. I soon realized that I could do whatever I wanted throughout the week because Sunday night was "grace" night. A little weeping and crying at the altar, mixed with confession, absolved my weekly sins. Monday was a new day. If I messed up during the week, it wasn't a big deal because Sunday night was coming.

My plan seemed workable. I could apply God's grace on Sunday for a week's worth of mess-up. Since God would forgive me, it didn't matter how badly I failed. Being "good" was hard work, and at times beyond what I thought even possible. After all, I was a teenager. Did anyone really expect me to be perfect? And Paul did say in Romans that where sin increases, so does grace. Our youth group provided God with multiple opportunities to extend grace!

As adults, many of us haven't grown much beyond this adolescent thinking. We have a similarly distorted view of grace. We still think it doesn't matter what we do because God's grace is a free pass. We use His gift to rationalize our behavior.

Cheap Grace Will Buy You a Costly Divorce

I know it's wrong to divorce, but God will forgive me.

Divorce is not the unpardonable sin.

It's OK to divorce. God's grace will cover me.

This logic has been applied to numerous marriages. Divorce is an intentional strategy used to end an unhappy relationship. After the divorce happens, talk about grace begins. In other words, divorce now and deal with it later. "Later" is all about what God will do. But what about what you will do prior to divorce? Can we talk about God's grace beforehand? When I try, I'm often rebuffed. Why? Because some people don't want to extend God's grace during difficulties—only after they've escaped them. Sound familiar? Then this chapter is for you!

Divorce is forgivable. No one will argue that point. And

Cheap Grace

God's grace does cover our sins. There are countless examples of this in the Bible. Grace is extended to murderers, slanderers, the greedy, the rebellious and the unjust—to name only a few. Hey, compared to murder, divorce hardly seems like a big deal. But grace is often misunderstood and certainly misapplied when we use it to justify our actions. Too many use grace as a license to be disobedient.

Grace Was Addy's Ticket Out

Addy wanted out of her marriage. She'd had it with Austin. He was a workaholic who pushed her to do more than she felt was reasonable. Addy was a successful motivational speaker booked regularly throughout the year. Austin felt Addy could make more money if he pushed her a little harder.

He pushed, and she let him. She agreed to the beefed-up schedule but grew exhausted and angry. Addy didn't tell Austin how she felt, but began to blame him for her unhappiness. She allowed resentment to build.

Little things started to bother her. As we learned in previous chapters, her resentment grew to feelings of contempt. Her recurrent thought was, *I don't deserve this. God wants me happy. I'm not happy. Austin is bullheaded. I can't fight him. I need out.*

When Addy came to therapy, she had already determined to leave Austin. She didn't want to discuss her role in their unhappiness drama—her inability to say no, agreeing to things when she didn't want to, keeping her feelings secret and warehousing resentment. Her problems were solvable if she would just admit to them. But like so many unhappy people, she didn't. She chose to blame her spouse and believed her only hope for happiness depended on escaping the relationship.

Addy and Austin were locked in a destructive pattern. He pushed; she silently agreed. He pushed more, and she built up resentment. The cycle continued until Addy checked out of the relationship emotionally–she no longer wanted to be married.

When Austin came to the session, he was blindsided by Addy's growing contempt for him. In the past months he had noticed her increased irritability and distance, but he assumed (incorrectly) that her behavior was due to extended family stress.

Addy told him, "You are always unaware of what is going on with me because you are so obsessed with success. I'm tired of you and this marriage. Nothing is going to change. And frankly I don't have the energy or desire for things to change. I'm leaving."

In a private session I asked Addy how she could take this position given her reported spiritual convictions. I understood her growing frustration and change in feelings, but I didn't understand her unwillingness to work on problems. The contempt she felt for Austin was, in part, her own doing. And Austin wanted to work on their problems.

But Addy was angry. "I know I'm not perfect, and you don't have to remind me of that. I prefer working on my problems alone. Austin is too overbearing and insensitive to women. He's old school–dominant and intrusive. I have friendships with men who understand me and are far more sensitive to my needs. Don't worry, nothing sexual has happened, but emotionally I see what I am missing. I know I shouldn't divorce, but God wants me happy and will forgive me. I'm not happy. Don't you believe God will forgive me? You and others always talk about God's grace. Well, now I'm in need of it, so I'm taking it. I want out. This isn't the unpardonable sin."

Sadly, Addy's view of grace has permeated Christian marriages–"I can use God's grace to do as I please." Usually the thinking runs like this: *I don't want to be married to this person anymore.* These are not cases of abuse, infidelity or abandonment. These are people who want out simply because of personal unhappiness. And their concept of God's grace is the ticket out.

I'll Take My Chances

Tom and Jane were on shaky ground. Tom was living alone in an apartment because he was having an affair with his girlfriend, Robin. Tom had no interest in reconciliation with his wife. Robin, also separated from her husband, was finishing the details of her own divorce.

Tom's wife, Jane, didn't want a divorce. She wanted her husband to come to his senses and give up the girlfriend. He was not interested in doing that. Instead, he wanted a divorce.

Tom's story is all too familiar. He'd been unhappy with Jane for years. They argued and "grew apart." (See Lie #4.) Meanwhile, Tom met Robin at work and began an intimate relationship with her. He believed he'd found his true "soul mate" and should leave his wife. Tom realized he didn't have biblical grounds, but claimed he was in love with another woman. So he told Jane he couldn't live without his newfound love.

Tom concluded his story and asked me, "Don't you think God has enough grace to cover me here? I know I shouldn't have had an affair. It just happened." (Sorry, affairs don't just happen—see chapter 10.) "Anyway, it's too late. I love Robin, and now I finally know what it's like to be in a loving relationship. I won't go backwards. I expect you and others to understand and extend grace to help me get through this."

Against my advice, Tom left his wife. He found a church that supported his decision and new friends who rationalized his behavior. He never repented to his wife or children. "Just get a better understanding of grace," he told them. He told me the same thing.

This application of grace is manipulative. To sin willfully, expecting God to cover it, is distorted. Tom was wrong to have an affair. He was even more wrong to continue it boldly. Still, God's grace was available if he were remorseful and repentant. Instead, he pursued the more immediate desire—his girlfriend. Not only did he break up his marriage and his girlfriend's marriage, but five children were also affected. Tom used grace to justify his actions. His willful disobedience was the issue that he refused to address.

I think of the many high-profile Christian marriages now joining the divorce ranks. I am disturbed by the reasons, at least the reasons publicly used, to justify divorce. They're all variations on a theme, the divorce theme: "It's best this way. God understands and wants me happy. It's God's will. We do better apart than together. Now I can relate to the pain of others. We made a mistake. We love each other, but we can't live with each other." It's all a pack of cultural lies. They bought it—and often, so do we.

The divorce excuses are just as off base as Christians' reactions to divorce: "Look, so-and-so is only human. Divorce isn't going to hurt his or her ministry in the long run. It's just not that big of a deal anymore. Lots of Christians get divorced. The church understands. Don't even give it a second thought. Divorce makes you a better person. We're only human. It's not a big deal."

It *is* a big deal.

We have learned to accommodate the culture. We've been desensitized to the destructive power of divorce. It happens so often, and so many people avoid being accountable to God—or anyone else. We have learned to rationalize behavior to fit our circumstances. Once the slide down that slippery slope into justification and compromise begins, we find ourselves allowing things we would never have tolerated before.

Then it is only a matter of time. Behavior follows beliefs.

Cheap Grace

We have let ourselves get comfortable with something God hates. We are convinced divorce is no big deal. The culture contends that divorce is no one's fault. It just happens (witness the "no-fault" phenomenon). Learn to live with it as a product of postmodernity. Christians believe this rhetoric.

Take the case of Darva Conger (please take it because it confuses me), the infamous woman who married a millionaire on TV only to quickly get an annulment. Appearing on the Geraldo Rivera show in July 2000, she was asked how she, a born-again Christian, could pose nude for *Playboy* magazine. (Even Geraldo could see the moral dilemma!) Her response, which I'm paraphrasing, was something like this: "Life is full of difficult decisions. Posing nude is between myself and God."

It appeared that she was counting on God to forgive her. And He will if asked. But then she added how proud she was of the nude photos and that she planned to release more over the Internet.

I about fell over. Most of us aren't posing nude for *Playboy*, but our attitude about divorce is similar: "I'll do what I want, and God will forgive me. I'm staking my eternal life on it!"

I remember watching a well-known television pastor announce on television that he and his wife of many years were separated. He went on to say that if he and his wife divorced, he would resign immediately. Regrettably, after several years, the divorce happened. It was a sad moment for the entire church body.

However, instead of resigning as he had promised, he announced to his congregation that he would stay on as senior pastor. According to Chuck Colson's *Breakpoint Commentary*, his church administrator then took the pulpit explaining that the pastor's divorce would now help him better relate to the congregation. His presumption was that the church would benefit by the pastor's failed marriage because now he understood the pain of divorce. The congregation stood and applauded.

Chuck Colson asked, "Have our churches become so accustomed to moral failure that we applaud it?"[1] I realize the congregation loves their pastor and wants him to stay. And God loves the pastor and his wife, too. That's not the point. More importantly, this is not a put-down of any pastor who has experienced the shame and pain of divorce.

The point is that our response to divorce or any moral failing should be grief. Divorce is an immense loss and a break of holy covenant. Can God use divorced people? Absolutely, and good can come out of the tragedy. That's God's way. But we don't applaud the tragedy. We must mourn the loss and then trust God to bring beauty from ashes.

Divorced people are not excluded from God's grace. No one is. Many people I know couldn't stop their divorces. They never wanted them. They did everything possible to avoid that ultimate outcome. But they married people who believed a lie—"It doesn't matter what I do; God will forgive me." Their partners turned away from God and chose their own way.

One woman who came to me for therapy explained that her separated husband was living with another woman. Their daughter was having a difficult time with this arrangement because her father and his new girlfriend attended her church. So the mother asked her husband not to flaunt his sinful lifestyle in front of his daughter, especially at church since it so disturbed their daughter. The father refused to stop attending church with his live-in girlfriend. He told his daughter she was too conservative. God didn't have a problem with what he was doing. He was separated now and could do as he pleased.

Totally confused, the daughter went to see her pastor for guidance on the issue. She was troubled by her dad's behavior because of the faith and values he had instilled in her at a young age. Now he was acting contrary to those beliefs.

The "help" from the pastor was outrageous, a sign of present thinking: "I know it must be hard for you to worship here with your father and his 'friend,' but his financial contributions to the church must be considered. Perhaps you need to extend a little grace to your father."

The dad informed me that his pastor's understanding of grace was far superior to mine. His tolerance was something from which I could learn. God's love and grace would cover the situation. I should get off his back about living with another woman. He planned on marrying her eventually anyway. And his daughter just needed to accept the current arrangement and practice God's grace.

I began this book with a startling fact—the church has a higher divorce rate than the unchurched. The obvious question is, Why? Where does the transforming, miracle power of Jesus Christ fit into the lives of Christians? Are we apathetic, lulled into complacency, deceived? Have we allowed lies to creep into our thinking until we no longer recognize them as such? Have we maintained our compassion for divorced individuals, but lost our conviction about the act?

Our *laissez-faire* attitude about divorce is wrong and a disservice to the body of Christ. This doesn't mean we are to be judgmental or self-righteous. I'm not asking people to place scarlet Ds on the doorposts of households. There are Christians who tried to prevent divorce and had an unwilling partner. Jesus didn't condemn divorced people. Neither should we. But we do need to get serious about *preventing* divorce. Just because it is so acceptable doesn't mean we should do it. Our response must be compassion for the divorced. But at the same time, we must do everything in our power to stop the act.

The argument often goes, "If you say divorce is wrong, you're being self-righteous and judging others." No, you are agreeing with God's Word. It is not your place to judge the hearts of others, but it's OK to support a biblical position. I find it amazing that so many Christians are quick to judge homosexuality but slow to take as adamant a position on divorce.

Reconciliation is possible because of Christ in us. If God's Word is true, and if nothing is impossible to those who believe, then divorce isn't inevitable. Unfortunately, if you take this view you might find yourself alone, unpopular and criticized.

There is *God's way* and then there is *every other way*. God's way doesn't always line up with the cultural flavor of the day. Today when you believe a biblical truth you are labeled intolerant, mean, narrow-minded, self-righteous. The current cultural view is that everyone should make decisions based on their own ideas of right and wrong. It's called *relativity*, the postmodern anthem. Christians can't think this way because we have a Book that outlines absolute truth. It doesn't change with time. What was truth "in the beginning" still stands as truth today.

Grateful for Grace

When marital failure occurs, be saddened. Don't parade it, celebrate it, use it as an empathy tool or diminish it as a moral issue. Grieve. Reflect on your own sin or the sin that has been aimed against you, and be grateful for grace. Then determine to do whatever it takes to divorce-proof your marriage.

I know we delight in God's grace and compassion, but we can't allow ourselves to slip into a dangerous acceptance of divorce as normative. Don't believe divorce just happens. It doesn't.

Divorce forces us to think long and hard about God's grace. Unfortunately many Christians advocate what Dietrich Bonhoeffer coined, "Cheap Grace." Cheap grace gives license to sin because God will forgive it. People forget that grace doesn't excuse sin. It is the provision for sin.

Truth #9

Receive God's grace with a repentant heart.

N o one is beyond needing God's grace. I am no better than anyone else—and neither are you. Sin is sin no matter what form it takes. We are all sinners in need of redemption. Consequently, we have all sinned and come short of the glory of God. Greed, pride, envy, covetousness, adultery, lies—who is without sin? Whether our sin is on public display or secretly hidden away doesn't matter. It exists. How we deal with our sin is the important message of this chapter.

Don't Throw Stones or Walk Away

Remember the story of the adulterous woman recorded in John 8? The Pharisees were about to stone her. They brought the woman caught "in the act" to the temple where Jesus was teaching. According to the Law, she faced death while the man went free (hardly a picture of gender equality). Anyway, the Pharisees tested Jesus, "Should she be stoned?"

Jesus responded, "He who is without sin among you, let him throw a stone at her first" (John 8:7). One by one her accusers slinked away. No one had a right to throw stones. Great story about grace, right? But there's more.

Jesus then asked the woman, "Where are those accusers of yours? Has no one condemned you?" (v. 10).

She replied, "No one, Lord."

Then Jesus said, "Neither do I condemn you; go and sin no more" (v. 11). He forgave her sin and warned her to stop committing adultery. She, who was caught in the act, didn't deny what she had done. Unlike the Pharisees, she didn't retreat. She stood in front of Jesus ready to "take her medicine." Rescued from death, she was grateful for anything. He offered His grace, grace that came *after* repentance.

I love the contrast between the religious crowd who denied their sin and the acknowledged sinner who did not. Grace was extended to the one who admitted guilt. It wasn't a license for more adultery. In fact, Jesus told her, "Sin no more."

Guilt is the emotion that brings us to the reality of sin. Once our eyes are opened, we can still hide and blame others. Or we can repent. That's when we are in a position to receive God's grace.

The Pharisees took a "righteous stand" but were hardly guiltless. They needed God's grace as much as the woman, but they walked away from it. When we choose our own way over God's, we are like the Pharisees. We see our sin, but choose to deny it.

We expect God's free gift of grace, but we don't want to turn from our sinful ways. Denial does not lead to healthy guilt and a consequent turning of direction. Denial keeps people stuck, moving in the same direction.

Love—Not the Club—Is the Motivator

Knowing what is sin doesn't always stop us from doing it. We count on the grace of God to cover us. We've all done this even though Paul warns us about it in Romans 6.

I've taken advantage of God's grace just because it was available. At those times I was not walking intimately with God. It was easy to bank on God's goodness when I distanced myself from Him.

In a healthy relationship, you want to please your

spouse and do good things for him or her. When you dated, you would do whatever you could because you loved and cherished your loved one. As a newlywed, your spouse didn't have to demand your affection. Your love flowed freely.

Our relationship with God is like that. God doesn't force our obedience. Oh, He tells us what will happen if we do or don't follow His ways. But we still have choices. Hopefully love is our motivation rather than the negative consequences. Love drives us to please Him, to appreciate the great sacrifice He made by sending His Son to die for us. And because of love, we desire to be like Him—holy.

Cheap grace is like saying to God, "Thanks for sticking with me. I'll come around when I'm ready, if I ever get ready. I know You'll be there waiting for me. In the meantime, I'll continue to sin knowing You've taken care of it."

When we sin, our Father isn't pleased, but He loves us anyway. Do we take advantage of that love and continue to sin? Or are we grateful for what God has done and make every effort to be more like Him?

When people tell me they want a divorce but know it's wrong, I ask about their relationship with God. In most cases, they've lost any sense of intimacy with Him. Having determined a course, they're not interested in God's opinions.

Grace Under Fire

John was ready to end his marriage to Kirsten, but he had no acceptable biblical reason. He just wanted out. He and Kirsten both came from Christian families where divorce was unthinkable. John's divorce would be the first divorce in his family. Desperate to get out of the marriage, he began telling lies about his wife. He hinted to friends that Kirsten was unfaithful. She wasn't.

Friends believed John's intimations. Sympathy followed. As

the lies grew and spread, no one questioned John's decision to leave the marriage. He knew he should stop the misunderstandings, but he didn't. He trusted that God would forgive him *after* the divorce. He would allow the lies to continue, get the divorce and then deal with his dishonesty.

Kirsten was devastated by John's decision to leave. She never understood his reasoning. Based on the lies he'd spread, her friends thought she was covering up, and they pulled away.

Six months after the divorce, John felt terrible about what he had done. He had allowed lies to circulate that condemned Kirsten's behavior and excused his. The guilt was too much to carry. He had to tell the truth and clear up the lies he'd promulgated.

John was shocked when he confessed and Kirsten forgave him. She suggested counseling. Despite being treated unfairly, she wanted to restore the marriage.

When people asked her why she would even consider reconciliation after being maligned, she simply replied, "I didn't deserve what Christ did for me, and He still did it. Now it's my turn to do the same." Kirsten's willingness to extend grace changed John. Never had anyone been so loving to him. For the first time in his life, he was able to understand God's love and grace. He knew he didn't deserve Kirsten's love, but she gave it to him anyway.

Many thought Kirsten was a fool. They called her a dependent woman who allowed John to walk all over her. Kirsten saw the relationship differently. "I know I was wronged, and it hurt tremendously. But I made a covenant with this man, and I'm not ready to throw it away because of his stupidity. If he can admit his mistakes and change, we have a chance to honor our commitment. That means more to me than anyone else's perception. I'm doing what I feel is right before God. I really don't care what other people think."

Cheap Grace

When you truly begin to understand God's amazing grace, your marriage will no longer sink to adolescent schemes about what you can get away with. Grace is not the ace up your sleeve for acting out. Motivated by love, you will want to please God in all you do, especially by honoring your marital covenant. If you want to divorce-proof your marriage, understand that grace is the provision for sin—not an excuse to continue it. Accept God's grace, and freely give it to your partner.

Review

Lie #9   *It doesn't matter what I do; God will forgive me.*

Truth #9   *Receive God's grace with a repentant heart.*

Divorce-Proofing Strategies

- Lose your adolescent view of grace.

- Don't deny your sin. Face it.

- Confess, repent and change.

- Don't use grace to justify your sin. It is the provision for sin.

- Don't be condemned. Appropriate God's grace correctly.

- Stay intimate with God.

- Have a grateful heart that shows gratitude through godly living.

- Be motivated by love to obey God.

- Accept God's grace, and extend it to your partner.

CHAPTER 12

Nothing
Is Impossible

Lie #10

*It's too broken. Nothing can fix
this relationship.*

Many couples stagger to a sad moment in their relationship when it feels that nothing can save the marriage.
They either feel utter contempt for their partner, or they are
convinced that the only solution for emotional health is
divorce.

They have given up. The future looks grim unless there is
drastic change. Without hopeful signs of change, separation
and divorce become ultimate solutions. They are tired of
fighting. There is too much bad history to overcome, or they
can no longer tolerate the spouse's behavior. They are "out
of love," have "grown apart" or "are too different." Marriage
was a mistake, came too soon, was chosen out of desperation
or became too confining. Whatever the reason, the belief is,

"It's just too late to make this work."

This may be reality if you look only at the circumstances and relationship issues. But there is more to consider. And that is where hope springs eternal. Without hope, troubled marriages face disaster.

From a Mess to a Miracle

Jenna was convinced she had to leave Kurt to survive. Years earlier, Jenna had been married to a Christian man, Danny, who eventually divorced her because of an affair. Deep pain accompanied that rejection. But life had to go on. She needed to establish a single-parent household for her two daughters. It was lonely work. Her ex-husband rarely came around. He was too busy dating other women.

The wound was especially hard for Jenna because her ex-husband continued in ministry. Apparently people didn't know the real story behind the breakup, and so he remained in a ministry position.

About a year after Jenna's divorce was final, a man in her singles' class at church asked her out. Feeling there was no hope of getting back with her first husband, Jenna accepted the invitation. She and her new friend Kurt started to date. Kurt had also divorced after his wife left with his best friend. His ex-wife and the best friend married two years later.

Obviously, Kurt and Jenna had much in common: loss and the pain of rejection. For six months they dated, seeing each other regularly. Neither had felt this good for years. Eventually Kurt asked Jenna to marry him. She accepted.

But six months into the marriage, Jenna felt she had made a huge mistake: "I married Kurt on the rebound." Every morning she woke up and thought, *I don't love this man. I'm afraid I only married him because I was hurting. Now what do I do?* Jenna felt trapped.

She tried to muster up feelings of affection for Kurt but

felt nothing. She began to avoid him at night, not wanting any physical involvement. In the evenings when Kurt came home from work, Jenna felt a blanket of depression cover her. She was irritable, ignored her husband and spent hours crying alone in her room.

Kurt tried to talk, wondering what he had done to upset her. Jenna didn't know what to say but finally blurted out, "I don't think I love you. I married you too soon and have no feelings for you. I made a terrible mistake." Kurt stared at her, shaken and mystified by what he was hearing. He loved Jenna and couldn't believe she felt that way.

"I've given this marriage one year and nothing is changing for me," Jenna continued. "I know we are Christians, but maybe we should admit this was a mistake and call it quits before we spend even more time together. How good can this be for my daughters if I'm depressed all the time?"

Kurt was speechless. Deeply wounded he flashed back to those old feelings of rejection from his first marriage. In desperation, he called an old friend who had helped him through his first divorce. The friend acknowledged that the marriage had happened rather quickly and that Jenna probably did not have enough time to process her loss. Her ex-husband was so kind each time he came to pick up the girls. Perhaps she was thinking about reconciliation. He counseled Kurt to be patient and not panic. Maybe Jenna was confused and just needed a little time to sort things out.

Jenna decided to see a therapist. Her depression was worsening, and she found herself constantly thinking about her ex-husband. In bed at night with Kurt, she wished it were Danny.

Then trouble. Danny told Jenna that his girlfriend recently left him. He paid extra attention to Jenna when he came for the girls, complimenting her and reminding her of private moments they shared during their ten years together. He was lonely now that he was without a woman. And he apologized for the way he had treated Jenna prior to their divorce.

Jenna never wanted to divorce Danny. Now that he said he was sorry, she was even more upset she had remarried. Her emotional isolation from Kurt grew exponentially. At night she wouldn't even talk to Kurt but waited by the phone for Danny to call about the girls. When Kurt questioned her loyalty, she became defensive and critical. "You don't trust me," she yelled. "I haven't done anything wrong." But her heart was unfaithful, fantasizing about times she and Danny made love.

Kurt asked Jenna to see a marital therapist with him. He was clueless how to win back her affection and deeply concerned with how agitated she was with him. The girls were noticing the friction and feared another divorce was coming. Jenna reluctantly agreed to see the therapist with Kurt. Perhaps she could explain the mistake she'd made marrying Kurt and the therapist would help her get a civil divorce. Secretly she harbored the hope Danny would court her again.

Then one day reality hit. Jenna called Danny to arrange visitation for the girls. A woman answered his phone. "I'd like to speak to Danny," Jenna continued. "Is he home?"

"No," the woman answered, "but I'll take a message."

"Are you the housekeeper?" Jenna inquired.

The woman laughed and said, "No, I'm much more than a housekeeper. We live together. I've been his girlfriend for the past six months. We are thinking of getting engaged."

Jenna dropped the phone. How could she have been so stupid? Betrayed again! Danny hadn't changed at all. Deceit was still a way of life for him. She had fallen for his lies a second time! Gasping for air she fled to her bedroom and slammed the door. "God, what is wrong with me? I'm so confused and feel so betrayed again." She knew she had to tell Kurt. Maybe he would leave her too, but she couldn't keep all this inside any longer.

At the next marital session, Jenna told Kurt about her secret hopes for a reconciliation with Danny. She confessed her devastation that he had again deceived her, never truly repentant for his behavior. She acknowledged not knowing how she felt toward Kurt. In fact, she wasn't even sure she could stay in this marriage either.

All this time Kurt's friend had quietly been talking to him about the lack of spiritual leadership in his home. The friend realized this unfilled role had played a part in the breakup of Kurt and his first wife. He met with Kurt every Saturday morning for prayer, encouraging him to get closer to God and ask for His wisdom with Jenna. Kurt had been searching the Scriptures and somehow kept reading how nothing is impossible with God. Feeling desperate to keep this marriage, he claimed that promise and began to intercede for his wife. One of his prayers was that anything hidden would come out into the open.

Jenna wasn't talking to God. She was still angry with Him and certainly afraid to talk about her feelings. God, she felt, abandoned her when Danny left. And the fact that he stayed in ministry was even more difficult to swallow. It wasn't fair. And why wasn't God taking her side? Now Danny had betrayed her again, and again with no consequences in sight.

The therapist spent time helping Jenna work through the issues of her divorce—the betrayal, the lying, the deceit, the repeated adultery. Jenna had never allowed herself to grieve those losses. She'd been too busy with the pain. She blamed herself for not being good enough. Then she blamed God. Her anger at God was intense. Jenna was never free to express anger toward her earthly father without a serious consequence, so she'd learned to keep the anger inside. Now her spiritual distance with God was similar to her father. "God can handle your angry feelings," her therapist reassured. "In fact, He's aware of them already."

Jenna had a right to feel angry, but avoiding God was not the solution. Alienation kept her away from the One who could help the most. As the therapist worked through the loss of the first marriage and helped Jenna deal with her anger over injustice, the confusion lessened. Her depression began to lift. Kurt reaffirmed his love for Jenna and how much he wanted this marriage to work. She wasn't so sure. Deep in her heart Jenna still believed this marriage had been a rebound. So the therapist asked, would she ask God to place a new love for Kurt in her heart? No need to pretend she loved him. All she had to do was be willing to allow a miracle to happen. If she wanted to honor her vow, God would help her find a way to love Kurt.

Jenna knew her answer required a step of faith. Feeling nothing for Kurt at the moment, she nonetheless agreed to try God. The couple's homework assignment for three months was to concentrate on nothing but strengthening their relationships with God: Read the Bible daily, spend time in prayer and worship. They were to list the promises of God and keep track of how He intervened in the lives of His followers as recorded in the Bible.

With sincere hearts, they agreed. Changes began to be evident. Kurt assumed his role as spiritual leader. He began praying with his wife, hungering after the things of God and filling his mind with the Word. The realization that he had never truly depended on God to help him through difficulties hit him hard. It had been his prideful self-reliance that had kept him from looking to God in times of trouble. He realized he used the failure of his first marriage as an excuse not to assume spiritual leadership in the home.

Jenna began to find herself. Her identity was tied to men. She longed for acceptance. But she didn't know who she was apart from being a wife. She read how she was God's child, constantly on His mind, holy and blameless in God's sight, redeemed, loved for who she is, reconciled to God, free from fear and never separated from His love. Her heart softened as she forgave those who had hurt her and released years of pent-up anger. Newly recognizing herself as God's child, Jenna was renewed and assured that:

- God loves her just as she is (John 3:16).

- She is righteous or "right with God" (Rom. 5:1).

- She is a complete person (Col. 1:28).

- She is God's handiwork (Eph. 2:10).

- God will never leave her or forsake her (Heb. 13:5).

- She is secure in her faith (John 10:28–30).

- She is free from all fears (Ps. 34:4).

- She need not fear any man. (Ps. 56:11).

- If she delights in God, He will give her heart's desires (Ps. 37:4).

- She has an abundantly rich life (John 10:10).

- She has been furnished with every good thing (Ps. 84:11).

- She has been freely given God's grace (Eph. 1:6).

- She has truth (John 16:13).

- She has strength for every situation (Isa. 40:31).

After three months of intense study and newfound intimacy with God, the couple returned to therapy. Jenna didn't know how it happened, but she was beginning to feel love for Kurt. In her words, it was nothing short of a miracle. She admired and respected his spiritual sincerity. And for the first time, she saw a man who honored his vow even when things were difficult. Kurt had not rejected her when she rejected him. He was a living model of God's love.

I could tell you numerous stories of couples who appeared hopeless when it came to staying together. Some have lived through dramatic life circumstances and problems. Others are more like Kurt and Jenna—wounded and hurt over past disappointments and rejection. They are deceived by the lie that nothing will fix their relationship. They've given up, feeling divorce is their only option.

Kurt and Jenna are not bad people. They're two wounded people making their way in life. If you think about it, we all fit this description to some degree. The biggest lie we can tell ourselves is that we don't need God to rule our hearts and minds. We can do it alone—rely on our talent, abilities, whatever. When our relationships falter, we easily succumb to the thinking of the culture. *It's too late. It's not working. Let's call it quits. It would take a miracle to fix this.* Good thing our God is in the miracle business!

Truth #10

It's never too late because nothing is impossible with God.

A gain, let me remind you, I am not trying to condemn those of you who have divorced over repeated adultery and unrepentant behavior that is harmful or dangerous. I am writing to those who have simply given up because you no longer feel love or can no longer see your way to a peaceful and loving relationship.

I'm asking you to examine your heart and then your beliefs. Do you believe in the God of the impossible? Will you allow Him to work a miracle in your heart and relationship? If you say no to this, then you probably will divorce. If God isn't big enough to do what He promises, who is? If God can't change hearts, who can? There has to be a willingness to submit to something bigger than you or a therapist.

Can anything resurrect a dead marriage? Yes, the miracle power of God can. But first you must understand what and with whom you're truly at war, and learn how to fight the real enemy. How? You transform your mind and act according to belief. Here's how.

Know Your Enemy and Do Battle

When you feel that you are at the end of the road and the next stop is divorce, remember who your real enemy is. It may seem that it's your spouse. He or she may be doing things that are hurtful, rejecting and angry. But the real enemy behind divorce is not a person. There is a bigger force trying to destroy what God has put together. It is a force of darkness. It is real and operates in an invisible world that exists all around us. You are about to do battle with a spiritual enemy.

How do you begin to war against the force behind all the unhappiness? First, believe there are principalities and powers operating against you. Second, clean up your act. Line up your thinking with God's. Get your behavior in line with godly living. Then begin to fill yourself up with the Word of God and His promises. Say them, rehearse them and claim them as yours. Your mouth has the power of life and death, according to the Bible. Confess life and new breath into your marriage. Confessing what God says about you and your situation brings new belief that it is true.

Next, do battle against those dark forces. Identify the spiritual roots of problems and attack them in the Spirit. For example, "I pray against that anger that is gripping my spouse. I have the authority to demand it go away in Jesus' name. I command it to go. Greater is He that is in me than he that is in the world. Anger, you have no authority in this house. I pray the peace of God over this place." Walk the floors, talk to God, take back what is yours by the authority given you in Jesus' name!

Even when you feel tired and defeated, remind yourself that it's not over until it's over. Command doubt to leave you. Rehearse God's track record in impossible situations. Enlist one or two fellow Christians who understand how to war against this enemy. Meet with them regularly for prayer. You also need to be under the mantle of an anointed pastoral staff that prays and intercedes on your family's behalf. Wrap up all your weariness and use it in prayer. "God, I am weak, but in my weakness You promised to be strong. Make me strong to fight. You have given me the power to defeat the enemy. I want to start using that power now."

Too many Christians are spiritual anorexics. They have access to a feast of power but restrict its use because they are ignorant of God's Word or mistakenly too afraid to move by His Spirit. Use the resources your good and trustworthy heavenly Father has given you to overcome lies and move in His power. You are sons and daughters of the King. Start claiming your inheritance.

God Is on Your Side

Samantha looked at me and said, "There is no way my husband will change. He's thinking of filing for divorce. He holds all the power. He has more money, better attorneys and people willing to lie for him. He has maligned me unfairly and is now accusing me of things that are untrue. Why do I feel like I'm going to lose it all?"

I reminded Samantha of the story of David and Goliath—bigger army, better battle gear, bigger giant who mocked and taunted the Israelites. It's not just a story for kids. Goliath was a formidable enemy. David should have been minced meat. But he wasn't. Why did David beat the giant? God was on his side.

Nothing Is Impossible

In 2 Kings 6, the great Syrian army surrounded the city. When Elisha's servant saw all the horses and chariots waiting to strike at them, he asked Elisha what they should do. The prophet's response was, "Do not fear, for those who are with us are more than those who are with them" (2 Kings 6:16). Elisha saw the enemy, but he also knew God was on his side. He prayed that his young servant's eyes would see the heavenly horses and chariots of fire surrounding their enemies.

When your marriage looks hopeless because one person won't change, open your eyes to the truth that God is with you. His promise is to be on your side no matter who or what comes against you. God has assigned His angels to watch over you. Believe that God is present and on your side. If He is for us, no one, no force, no thing can win against us.

Samantha's challenge was to maintain a godly response to her husband. True, she wanted to get revenge, expose his lies and ruin his reputation. She had every right. But she chose the armor of God instead of the ways of the world. Rather than anger, revenge and ruin, she chose peace, righteousness, faith and the Word. She knew God would help her even though the odds were against her. She prayed. Daily, she pictured the angels hovering over her. She believed God would fight for her. Somehow, miraculously, her husband would see the need for change.

You can operate in the same confidence as Samantha. God is on your side. Go to Him when you feel overwhelmed and need a victory. Stand firm on His Word, and believe He is there, ready to fight for you. Remember, you can't make your spouse change (see chapter 6), but you can pray and believe that he or she will see the need to change. This isn't a wimpy strategy. Prayer and intercession are powerful.

You Are Not Condemned

If you are the one who has strayed and turned your back on

the things of God, He wants you back. He is waiting with loving arms. If you repent, you are not judged. Are you tired of feeling judged and condemned for the things you did in the past? Do you regret wasting so much of your life involved with drugs, alcohol and unholy living? Do you have trouble forgiving yourself of an abortion, an affair or acts of immorality? The good news is you don't have to feel this way any longer. So many fail to realize the power of the blood covenant over past sins. Yes, you know Jesus died on the cross to take your sin, but for some reason, you can't get past your mistakes. Consequently, you walk around carrying tremendous guilt and shame unnecessarily.

Guilt is not productive unless it relates to sin conviction. You *should* feel guilty when you violate God's Word. But once you have acknowledged your sin and repented, you are no longer judged or condemned. Too many don't repair relationship problems because they can't believe God is not judging or condemning them.

Jesus does not accuse you to the Father. He says so in John 5:45: "Do not think that I shall accuse you to the Father; there is one who accuses you—Moses, in whom you trust." What He is saying here is that we can never measure up to the Law of Moses. All of us sin and fall short of living a perfect life.

When Jesus came, He took our failings to the cross and became the ultimate failure for us. His blood sacrifice now covers all our failings. Today we live under grace—not law. Therefore, when we make mistakes, we are no longer condemned by the old law, but justified through Christ. We need to understand this.

Our accuser is the devil (Rev. 12:10). He is the one telling us we are no good, unworthy of the blood of Jesus. He continues to throw lies at us, penetrating our thinking until we believe that we deserve to be judged.

We fight the accuser by resisting him. He has been thrown

down and is under our feet. Many of us were taught that the Holy Spirit lives in us to convict us of sin. This would mean He is an accuser. Since He is part of the Holy Trinity, this is untrue. He convicts us of unbelief. He wants us to know and believe the Word. When Jesus says we are not accused, the Holy Spirit reminds us of His Word so we can stand in truth—we are no longer judged or condemned.

This doesn't mean we go on sinning. Sin leads to death. It means when we sin, we repent and then know and believe that our sin is gone. When we truly believe this, we no longer live in condemnation. So drop that unhealthy guilt and shame. Jesus does not accuse you. Stop accusing your-self. Stop listening to the real accuser—Satan. He wants you stuck in guilt and shame. Jesus wants you free.

Seek Him and You Will Find Him

When my children were little, we liked to play hide-and-seek. The kids loved the game. One time when it was our daugh-ter's turn to hide, we couldn't find her. She picked a terrific hiding spot. At first, we were challenged by her ingenuity. Later, frustrated we eventually gave up looking. "Game over," we yelled. "Time to show yourself." She squealed with delight that no one could find her.

You know, we tend to think God likes to play hide-and-seek. We run into a problem and try to deal with it. When it doesn't resolve quickly or to our liking, we think God has abandoned us and can't be found. We think God has gone into hiding. We say to ourselves, "God doesn't care about me. He's obviously interested in helping others, but not me." We give up and get depressed. The truth is, God isn't hiding. He is ever present and can always be found. It's His great pleasure to help you.

The problem for most of us is that we act as if God isn't there. Our natural inclination is to do things our way. If our way doesn't work, we might turn to God. Then again, if we're stubborn, we may just try another solution. Finally, at our wits' end, we might give God a try.

David faced a crisis situation and decided to seek God. In 1 Samuel 30, the Amalekites attacked the city of Ziklag. They burned it and kidnapped all the women, children and livestock. When David and his army, exhausted from battle, arrived and saw the destruction, he and his army wept. The city was destroyed, and their wives and families were gone to who knew where. The situation was ripe for mutiny. In their agony and despair, the men took a vote to stone David.

But pay attention to David's response to his very grim circumstances. He asked God what he should do next. God spoke, "Pursue, for you shall surely overtake them and without fail recover all" (1 Sam. 30:8). What was David's response to an agonizing crisis? He asked God what to do about it. And God answered. He was present, ready to answer. Moreover, it was God's plan for David and his army to recover all that was lost—more evidence of what a great God we serve.

If we seek God, He will show us what to do. If you need an answer, ask Him to give you one. Don't give up if the answer isn't immediately evident. Sometimes we have to wait on the Lord and not grow weary. But the point is the Lord is always with you, a present help in the time of trouble. He will speak to you if you ask. He should be the first person consulted, not the last.

If you seek God, you will find Him (2 Chron. 15:2). He isn't watching at a distance like the Bette Midler song suggests. He is not uninvolved, sitting in heaven playing hide-and-seek. He is waiting to have an intimate relationship with you. Seek Him and you will find Him.

Tune In to His Frequency

Do you realize that God is always talking to us? Be encouraged. We are His sheep. He is the Good Shepherd. His Word says if we listen for His voice, we will hear it. How do we hear the voice of God? Think of it like this: Pretend God is on a specific frequency on the radio. He is there ready to be heard if we will tune to the right station. We must learn to adjust ourselves to hear what He is ready to say.

Too many people get discouraged and depressed because they think God speaks to others and not to them. God is not a respecter of persons. What He does for others, He will do for you.

One way to prepare yourself to hear the voice of God is keep your heart soft to the things of God. You should soak in the Word of God, stay repentant and forgiving and walk in humility.

A hardened heart keeps us from hearing God's voice. Here are four things you can do to stay soft and ready to hear God's voice:

1 We have an inheritance from God that we need to "boast" about according to the Bible. Proclaim what is yours because of the sacrifice of Jesus Christ. *Be confident in what God has told you in His Word, and speak those things.* The opposite of confidence is being unsure of what is rightfully yours. We have a rich Father who wants to bless us if we believe and confidently proclaim His blessings.

2 *Stop testing God.* Faith comes from *hearing* the Word, not *seeing* immediate results (Heb.11:1). One way to harden your heart is to do what the Israelites did. They constantly questioned God even after He performed mighty miracles for them. Stop wondering if God's promises are for you. Because you are a joint heir with Christ, you can know that He will be faithful to do all things.

3 The Bible has much to say about unbelief. Unbelief

stopped Jesus from doing miracles in His home-
town. The Bible even goes so far as to say someone
with unbelief has "an evil heart." In Mark 16:14,
Jesus rebuked unbelief and hardness of heart. *God
wants you to believe what He says* even when you
don't see immediate evidence. This pleases God.

4 Be careful not to be carried away by your own lust
and sin. *Don't willfully reject the Word that tells you how
to behave and do good.* When you allow sin to stay
present in your life, you allow interference in the
radio waves of God's voice.

A soft heart is more amenable to hearing God's voice.
Take time to listen to a God who wants to speak to you.

Believe in the God of the Possible

Perhaps the biggest obstacle of all is unbelief. If you don't
believe God can work in your life for good, that God only
wants what is best for you and that His ways are higher than
your ways, then you won't submit to Him.

God your heavenly Father is perfect, loves you unconditionally and has good things planned for you. But if you really
don't buy this and see Him as a bad guy ready to punish you
or as someone distant (or some other distorted view), you will
never believe He can change you into something incredible.
You also won't believe He is the God of the impossible.

Let's look at several biblical examples. In Genesis 18, Sarah
laughed when she overheard she would finally have a baby.
She was old and way past childbearing years. God's response
to her laughter was to ask why she was laughing. God knew.
He didn't have to ask. It's almost as if He says, "Sarah, what
is up with you? Don't you know that I am the God of the
impossible? Yes, in the natural this would be foolishness, but
I am God. I speak My Word, and it happens."

Nothing Is Impossible

In the last chapter of Job, after Job suffers much and has been tested, he says about God, "I know that You can do everything, and that no purpose of Yours can be withheld from You" (Job 42:2). In the face of hopelessness, Job had hope in God.

Jeremiah 32:17 reminds us, "Ah, Lord GOD! Behold, You have made the heavens and the earth by Your great power and outstretched arm. There is nothing too hard for You." Those words were repeated when the angel came to the virgin Mary announcing she would bear a son, as would her cousin Elizabeth, "For with God nothing will be impossible."

When the disciples were not successful casting out demons in Matthew 17, Jesus teaches them about faith. He says, "If you have faith as a mustard seed, you will say to this mountain, 'Move from here to there,' and it will move; and nothing will be impossible for you" (v. 20). Through His power we too have the ability to do impossible things.

We are reminded in Romans 4:18 that in hope against hope, Abraham believed. You need to have hope, not in circumstances or other people, but in the things of God. Faith is the substance of things *hoped* for. Believe in God. He can work an impossible situation because of who He is.

My pastor reminds me that most of us live in the *probable*. We *probably* won't get better. We *probably* will be divorced. We will *probably* have money problems. We *probably* . . . (fill in the blank). Instead, we should live in the *possible*. All things are possible with God. His plans for us are good. He gives us a hope and a future.

Renew your mind with the possibilities of God. No circumstance is beyond His help because of who He is. When you feel down, discouraged or hopeless, remember the God of the *possible*. What He has done for others, He can do for you. Place your hope in God, and He will turn the situation around.

The road that leads to divorce begins in the mind and heart. If we listen to the lies of the culture, we begin to believe the lies all around us. Then we find ourselves wandering into dangerous territory. The lies build. They work on our feelings and eventually affect our perception of our relationship. It isn't long until those lies lead us to "fall out of love" or to "grow apart."

Protect your marriage from divorce. Resist the lies of the culture with the truth of God's Word. Divorce doesn't have to happen. You and your partner can prevent divorce if you recognize the cultural lies, keep your relationship with God and each other strong, believe His promises apply to you and live according to His plan.

If you stay intimately connected to God, your marriage will reflect intimacy. God wants you to honor your marital covenant. Use this book to help you achieve that end. Begin to divorce-proof your marriage today.

Review

Lie #10	*It's too broken. Nothing will fix this relationship.*
Truth #10	*It's never too late because nothing is impossible with God.*

Divorce-Proofing Strategies

- Know your enemy, and prepare for battle.
- Remember God is on your side.
- Don't live in condemnation.
- Seek Him, and you will find Him.
- Tune in to His frequency.
- Soften your heart to the things of God.
- Believe in the God of the possible.

Notes

INTRODUCTION
DIVORCE-PROOFING YOUR MARRIAGE

1. Source obtained from the Internet: Barna Research Online, www.barna.org/cgi-bin/PageCategory.asp?CategoryID=20, Family–Research Archives–Divorce (1999)

CHAPTER 2
THREE KEY PRECONDITIONS TO DIVORCE-PROOFING

1. Harriet Lerner, *The Dance of Anger* (New York: Harper & Row Publishers, 1985).

CHAPTER 3
ESCAPE AND AVOIDANCE

1. Jeff Wright, "Bill lets couples seek 'covenant marriages,'" *The Register-Guard*, Eugene, Oregon, May 18, 1999, front page.

CHAPTER 5
RESCUE FANTASIES

1. John Gottman, "Why marriages fail," *The Family Therapy Networker* (May/June 1994): 41–48.
2. Lerner, *The Dance of Anger*, n.p.
3. John Gottman, "Why marriages fail," n.p.

CHAPTER 6
DEALING WITH CONFLICT

1. John Gottman, "Why marriages fail," n.p.

CHAPTER 7
GROWING APART

1. Gottman, "Why marriages fail," 41–48.
2. Ibid.
3. Ibid.
4. Ibid.
5. Ibid.

6. Ibid.
7. Pat Love, "What is this thing called love?" *The Family Therapy Networker* (March/April 1999): 34–44.
8. Ibid.
9. Love, "What is this thing called love?": n.p.

CHAPTER 8
GENDER RELATIONS

1. Cheryl Rampage, "Gendered Aspects of Marital Therapy," *Clinical Handbook of Couple Therapy*, ed. Neil S. Jacobson and Alan S. Gurman (New York: The Guildford Press, 1995), 261–262.
2. Philip Yancey, *The Jesus I Never Knew* (Grand Rapids, MI: Zondervan, 1995), n.p.
3. John Gottman and Nan Silver, *The Seven Principles for Making Marriage Work* (New York: Three Rivers Press, 1999), 105.
4. R.T. Hare-Mustin and J. Marecek (Eds.), *Making a Difference: Psychology and the Construction of Gender* (New Haven: CT: Yale University Press, 1990).
5. Gottman, "Why marriages fail," 45–47.

CHAPTER 10
INFIDELITY

1. E. Laumann, J. Gagnon, R. Michael and S. Michaels, "The social organization of sexuality: Sexual practices in the United States" (Chicago: University of Chicago Press, 1994).
2. Ibid.
3. K. Choi, J. A. Catania, M. M. Dolcini, "Extramarital sex and HIV risk behavior among U.S. adults: Results from the national AIDS Behavioral Survey," *American Journal of Public Health* 84 (1994): 2003–2007.
4. S. R. Beach, E. N. Jouriles, K. D. O'Leary, "Extramarital sex: Impact on depression and commitment in couples seeking marital therapy," *Journal of Sex and Marital Therapy* 11 (1985): 99–108.

CHAPTER 11
CHEAP GRACE

1. "High Profile Divorce: The Cost of Biblical Faithfulness," *Breakpoint* with Chuck Colson, Commentary #000613, June 13, 2000.

Experience the Power of Spirit-Led Living

"In all thy ways
acknowledge Him and
He shall direct thy paths."
—Proverbs 3:6